CHRISTIANS, POLITICS, AND THE CROSS

Christians, Politics, and the Cross

*An Urgent Plea for the
Church to Return to Its Mission*

Erwin W. Lutzer

Moody Church Media
Chicago

CHRISTIANS, POLITICS, AND THE CROSS
Copyright © 2020 by Erwin W. Lutzer
Published by Moody Church Media
Chicago, Illinois 60614
www.moodymedia.org

ISBN: 9798602925869

CONTENTS

WELCOME TO CHRISTIANS, POLITICS, AND THE CROSS

The prediction was both astonishing and accurate.

One hundred years before Hitler rose to power, poet Heinrich Heine assessed the mood in Germany in his book, *The History of Religion and Philosophy in Germany.* He concluded that only Christianity and the cross of Christ were holding back what he called the "brutal Germanic love of war."[1] This prediction was even more remarkable because Heine was a Jew not a Christian; a man who, nevertheless, believed that only the cross could tame that warlike tendency.

Heine, who didn't understand the true meaning of the power of the cross, called it a talisman, an object with magical power that held aggression at bay in Germany. But he knew that should that cross be broken, the forces of brutality would break out, filling the world with "terror and astonishment."[2]

Parallels between Nazi Germany and the United States

can be easily overdrawn, but Heine's assessment might be just as applicable to us as it was to pre-war Germany. Under Hitler, the cross of Christ was broken and formed into a *hakenkreuz* (hooked or broken cross) that became a symbol of the Nazi agenda and replaced the cross of Christ in the German churches. This confusion of crosses beguiled the German church and invited the judgment of God. What if it is true to say about America, as Heinrich Heine said about Germany, that only the cross of Christ is keeping the country from self-destruction that, if left unchecked, would cause the whole world to be astonished? Do we not already see such forces at work in the disintegration of everything previously valued? We are living at a time when that which was once celebrated is now being condemned, and that which was condemned is now being celebrated.

My friends, the America we once knew is already gone.

As a nation, we are polarized both morally and politically. Yes, politics is important. Just consider the difference between North and South Korea. I asked a pastor from South Korea if he knew anything about the church in communist North Korea. He replied that, as far as he knew, the churches had not survived; a few believers just meet in homes secretly. There can be no evangelism, no outreach, and no measurable growth. However in South Korea, where freedom exists, evangelicals reportedly make up more than 20% of the population. There is a big difference between a political regime that squelches freedom and a political regime that allows freedom. Let no one say that politics is unimportant.

I do not believe, however, that politics is *most* important. Christians have a message which can actually transform lives; it is a message of hope for this world and great anticipation for the world to come. The message of the cross must stand above politics, economics, and culture. It is a transnational message that should be unaffected by geography, ethnicity, and/or political affiliations.

I ask those of us who are committed Christians: have we forgotten that God's power is more clearly seen in the message of the cross than in any political or social plan we might devise? Might not our desperate search for some antidotes to our grievous ills be symptomatic of our lost confidence in the power of the gospel to change people from the inside out? Do we cling to the cross with deep conviction that it is not simply a part of our message, but correctly understood, the whole of it?

Incredibly the church has, for the most part, abandoned the very message that is most urgently needed at this critical hour of history. At a time when we desperately need to engage our culture with the one message that has any hope of transforming it, many among us have pushed aside the cross in order to fight the world on its own terms and with its own strategies.

The message of the cross can be lost amid competing agendas. Ask any average American what Christians believe and you'll get multiple answers, some correct, others misleading. Few will say that the central doctrine of Christianity is that Christ came into the world to save sinners.

We are tempted to think that this time in history is unique for Christians. But the fact is that the disciples had all of our national woes times ten. Let me remind you that without any political base, without a voting bloc in the Roman Senate, and without as much as one sympathetic Roman emperor, they changed their world, turning it "upside down" as Luke says (Acts 17:6).

Yes, a favorable political structure can be a great boost to the church, but a lack of support is not fatal to the church's calling and mission. Even in North Korea and oppressive Muslim lands, at least a few Christians have survived and the message of the cross still changes lives. Their numbers might be small, but the gospel works even in the midst of persecution. This is a good time to remind the church to "cling to the old rugged cross."

TWO PREMISES

This book is based on two fundamental premises. First, we cannot retreat in the face of moral and spiritual opposition. Retreating is an admission of defeat. We cannot retreat even though we live in a culture determined to impose a destructive agenda on our children, our families, our churches, businesses, and every other strata of society.

We cannot run and hide. Ask the parent whose child is indoctrinated into the morally bankrupt LGBTQ worldview and is told that any opposition to their agenda is bigoted, homophobic, or worse. Ask the parent whose child is expected to participate when a drag queen reads a fairy tale in the local library. Ask the pastors who are afraid to have weddings in their churches, fearing that they will be forced to make their facilities available for homosexual weddings. In these and countless other ways, radical leftists will find us and try to force us to bow to their skewed view of reality.

The radical left is "in our face," so to speak, and we must resist them. We cannot simply withdraw to our Sunday schools and Bible conferences, witnessing as best we can while abandoning the world to its well-deserved fate. The activists are on a march and we cannot ignore them. There are battles to be won (or lost) and territory that must be conquered.

The second premise of this book is that yes, we must stand, but we must stand on biblical ground. We must see our battle not just as political or moral, but doctrinal and spiritual. Behind our political and moral conflicts is a spiritual realm that only the church can understand through the lens of Scripture. Although we might be able to elect politicians who enact laws that forbid certain kinds of moral perversity and fight for our eroding freedoms, no law or politician can rescue the United States from its spiritual freefall.

Better politicians should bring about better laws, but under no circumstances can politics do what the church can; politics can limit or promote certain behaviors, but it cannot change the heart. We need good politicians and better laws, but we need the gospel even more.

The willing blindness of our culture can only be explained when we realize that our battle is not just against our fellow Americans. As Paul put it, "For we do not wrestle against flesh and blood, but against the rulers, against the authorities, against the cosmic powers over this present darkness, against the spiritual forces of evil in the heavenly places" (Ephesians 6:12).

Cosmic powers! Spiritual forces!

Our so-called culture war is really a spiritual war. It is simply wrongheaded to expect that through political power we can "cleanup" America, ending the clamor for more homosexual rights, the imposition of transgenderism on our schools, the proliferation of trash television, and the love affair our nation has with violence and perversity. No. Let me be clear: no law can free us from the destructive influence of pornography and other morally debilitating addictions or actions.

Herein is the danger. We can become so overburdened with social/political agendas that the message of the cross is lost amid these skirmishes. Thus, the message of the cross that is presented to our culture loses its power because its message is clouded with political, social, and psychological agendas. The cross must always have its own space, its own center, its own exalted position.

We dare not approach the cross with cool detachment. The cross of Christ exposes the futility of our self-righteousness; it reminds us that we are sinners incapable of bringing about our own reconciliation with God. Before this cross we can only stand with bowed heads and a broken spirit.

And herein comes the warning. P.T. Forsyth, when speaking of the cross as the focal point of God's work for sinners wrote, "If you move faith from that centre, you have driven the nail into the church's coffin. The church, then is doomed to death, and it is only a matter of time when she shall expire."[3] The church can only live and breathe at the cross; without it there is no life and no reason to exist.

This book is written to encourage every single Christian to become involved in the conflict for the soul of this nation. We must begin with earnest prayer and fasting, but we cannot stop there. We must educate our children to discern the difference between righteousness and perversity;

we must teach them that human love and compassion can never be a substitute for what God has written in His Word. Without every Christian engaged in the conflict (in different ways, of course) it will be impossible to hold the forces of darkness at bay.

The cross that saved us must be gladly carried. And until we are willing to humbly carry this cross into the world, often at great personal cost, every victory will be fleeting and superficial. If there is any really good news in the world, we must proclaim it. What that good news is and how it must be proclaimed is the purpose of this book.

The great Charles Spurgeon said, "There is no cure for midnight but the rising sun...Shine forth, O Sun of Righteousness, and mist, and cloud, and darkness must disappear."[4]

Let us march ahead under the banner of "The Crucified."

Footnotes

1. Heinrich Heine, https://en.wikiquote.org/wiki/Heinrich_Heine

2. Heinrich Heine, *The Works of Heinrich Heine, Volume 5* (London: William Heinemann, 1892), 206.

3. P.T. Forsyth, *The Work of Christ* (London: Hodder & Stoughton, 1910), 53.

4. Charles H. Spurgeon, *Spiritual Parenting* (New Kensington, PA: Whitaker House, 2003), 118.

CHAPTER ONE

THE CLASH OF CROSS AND CULTURE

The cross has always clashed with popular culture.

Our present moral, political, and spiritual crisis is nothing new. Christians have always struggled with their role in culture, politics, and religion. At a time when the very religious and moral foundations of America are being dismantled, we need both direction and hope. We are not just in a temporal fight but one with implications for all of eternity.

Let us take a deep breath and learn a lesson from history.

Come with me to Rome in AD 410. As the city sits majestically along the Tiber River, its citizens stir to begin a new day quite confident that the future will be much like the past. Rome has, after all, lasted for 800 years so there's no reason to think that it won't continue for another 800.

Upon waking on the morning of August 24, the citizens were startled to discover that traitors were within their gates. During the night, Alaric, the first king of the

Visigoths, had overpowered the guards at the Salarian gate and filled the streets with his troops. At dawn the looting began.

The barbarians trashed the city, smashing works of art, hoarding treasure, and harassing the citizens. Most disheartening for the Roman citizens was the participation of their slaves in the looting. The powerless Romans could do little more than watch, feebly protesting the invasion.

When the Goths left three days later, their carts were loaded with gold, silver, and works of art. The city had not been burned, only punished; not destroyed, but humiliated. Some leaders had been killed but, for the most part, Rome could still function. The city was crippled, but not devastated. Jerome, the great historian, remarked that "the city which had taken the whole world was itself taken."[1]

BLAME THE CHRISTIANS

Quite naturally the question arose, "Who is to blame?" The citizens sought for a scapegoat, a reason why such a humiliation could have occurred. Their fingers pointed toward the Christians. This was, after all, their city.

To understand this accusation, we must turn the clock back one hundred years before this humiliating invasion. In AD 312, just before Constantine crossed the Milvian Bridge to sack Rome, he saw a cross of light in the heavens bearing the inscription, *In Hoc Signo Vinces,* "in this sign thou shalt conquer." He interpreted this vision as the sign of Christ's cross, so he marched his soldiers to the river and had them baptized as Christians. The cross was then emblazoned on their shields, and the soldiers went forth to conquer in the name of Christ.

Constantine, encouraged by his mother, Helena, promoted Christianity, believing that Christianity might unify the empire, providing a new force that would save classical culture and the empire itself. Indeed, he saw religion as so important that he gave the opening speech at the famous Council of Nicaea which was convened to hammer out the doctrine of the deity of Christ. He was not a theologian and cared little for the finer points of Christology. But he told the delegates that doctrinal division was worse than war; he wanted the church to be unified so that the empire could be unified. By the next generation, Rome was Christianized.

Conflict arose between the pagans and the Christians.

How did the pagans accept the Christian takeover? As we might guess, they resented it. In point of fact, many of them continued to hold to their pagan beliefs, refusing to conform to Christianity even outwardly; they clung to their pagan ideas, believing that their own gods were just as helpful as the God of the Christians. Others simply added Christian doctrines to those they already held, bringing paganism into the church, with the church often accommodating them. For example, they believed in many gods, each serving a different function; they had a god to invoke when they wanted to sell an object, another god when they wished to buy an object, and yet another when they took a journey, and so on. With the coming of Christianity, they could not continue to be polytheists, but their "gods" could retain their function if they were thought of as saints to whom the faithful could pray. Now when they took a journey, they prayed to St. Jude or St. Christopher, etc. Needless to say, for many, their conversion to Christianity was external only.

With Rome humiliated by the Goths, there was backlash against the imposition of Christian doctrine. The populace rose up saying their own pagan gods would have done a better job of defending Rome than the Christian God. Indeed, Rome became great under the dominion of pagan deities. The Christian God stood idly by, watching the barbarians ram the gate, and did nothing. Could a God like that actually be trusted? This was Rome, the center of Christendom. If the Christian God was all-powerful, why did He not intervene to defend His city? Why should the Christian gospel be proclaimed if the Christian God was indifferent to the plight of those who were called by His name?

Christianity faced a crisis in confidence.

Today we find ourselves in the same position as the Roman Christians. We are also being blamed for everything that is wrong with America: racism, bigotry, and the suppression of the poor. We are seen as the obstacle to the "fairness" and "progress" that would supposedly come with socialism and open borders. We are criticized for our narrow theological views that insist that Jesus is God and is the only way to the God the Father. But Christianity faced the same attacks centuries ago.

Augustine, the great Christian thinker, replied to the pagan critics of his day.

THE CITY OF GOD

Let's get the big picture before we give some specifics.

To defend Christianity, Augustine wrote *The City of God* in an attempt to vindicate "the glorious city of God against those who prefer their own gods to the Founder of that City." This "glorious city" was not Rome, but an eternal city God was building. Augustine defended the God of the Christians, insisting that the sack of Rome did not reflect unfavorably on His character. God has more important purposes than keeping the city of Rome intact. As a matter of fact, Rome was a wicked city and the invasion was justified, even on human terms.

Specifically, Augustine said, there are *two* cities, the city of God and the city of man. The city of man is built by men and reflects human dreams, hopes, and pride. This city is earthly, temporal, and capable of being destroyed. It will, in fact, eventually be totally obliterated.

There is, however, another city: the city of God. This city endures forever; this is the kingdom of God that gives meaning to the world; this is the city of the patriarchs and prophets, the city of the apostles and the church. This was the city "which hath foundations, whose builder and maker is God" (Hebrews 11:10, KJV).

Two different cities means two different citizens. The city of man is populated by those who live by their own laws. They are self-seeking, materialistic, and earthbound. They live their lives according to the rules of fallen human nature. To them, the destruction of Rome was a great catastrophe.

In contrast, the city of God comprises true Christians who follow God's laws and values. The citizens see beyond the earthly to the heavenly. To them, the destruction of Rome was not a travesty. In fact, the pillage of this earthly city could not deprive them of anything that had real value because their treasure was in heaven, out of reach of the barbarians.

These citizens set their sights on the unseen spiritual world which has a higher priority than the temporal, for God stands above history as we know it, He is not bound by the course of human events. These are followers of the cross, not beholden to emblems of human government.

These two cities can never be allies, for they represent two different origins, goals, values, and kings. "By two cities I mean two societies of human beings, one of which is predestined to reign with God for all eternity, the other doomed to undergo eternal punishment with the Devil."[2] In eternity past, only the city of God existed; since the fall of man, the two cities coexist; in the future they will be separated, each with its own eternal destiny. Our present responsibility is to live in both cities, giving each its due; we must give to Caesar that which is Caesar's and to God that which is God's.

Augustine did not mean that the city of man is destitute of all civil righteousness and justice. Yes, pagans have built great civilizations, thanks to the virtues they inherited as beings created in the image of God. Indeed, Christians should be actively involved in the city of man, building it, maintaining it, and working alongside those headed to destruction. But Christians should have no illusions about building an earthy utopia, for they must pass this life with continual opposition from the citizens of the city of man. They must march through the crumbling empires of the world, spreading the gospel.

We have a dual responsibility as citizens of the city of man and, more importantly, as citizens of the city of God.

AMERICA: THE CITY OF MAN

America's foundations are being attacked.

Statues of our Founding Fathers, our national heroes, are being toppled in an attempt to delegitimize America's Christian heritage. The argument goes that since some of the Founding Fathers had slaves, everything they did is to be rejected, undone, and even vilified. There is pressure to shift America's foundation from its Judeo-Christian roots and rebuild it on a "tolerant" secular foundation.

In the United States, the city of man is built on political correctness, the attempt to shame all those who disagree with the progressive left's banner of so-called "diversity." We have drifted into radical individualism, inflamed racial division, the privatization of religion, and increasing hostility to Christianity. Because objective truth is deemed nonexistent, what we choose for ourselves becomes the truth for us and shouldn't be questioned. Those who shout the loudest about the need for tolerance are often more intolerant than any fundamentalist would ever be.

The pagan values these radicals hold are now being imposed on everyone through legislation and cultural pressures. You and I know that religious freedom cannot be tolerated in a country where the city of man is in ascendancy. Thus the "wall of separation" between church and state is pressed into service to curtail religious expression at every level. Christians are expected to celebrate that which, at one time, was condemned.

Imagine a host of people sailing together on a ship. Some of the travelers insist that they have a right to drill a hole in the bottom on their side of the vessel. Indeed, they have their "rights" they tell us, guaranteed by the Constitution. Those on the other side of the ship are also respectful of freedom, but shout, "Remember we are on this ship too! Your 'freedom' could mean our collective doom!" Thus, there is conflict between the rights of individuals and the rights of the larger community.

It is not easy for us to watch the disintegration of our culture; it is not easy to see religious freedom eroded. With the First Amendment turned on its head and interpreted in ways the Founding Fathers would never have dreamed possible, freedom of speech is being taken away in every area of public life. School teachers are telling children that they cannot write papers on the topic of religion; even the word *God* is stricken from some textbooks. If that isn't bad enough, expansive rights are being given to pornographers, abortionists, and the LGBTQ lobby.

What do we do?

Augustine would tell us that we can expect this kind of opposition from the world. We must see this not merely as a political and cultural battle, but a spiritual attack that must be resisted. We can't depend on the weapons of the world. As I already emphasized in the introduction, we must see beyond the physical world to the invisible world where battles are won or lost.

Membership in the city of God empowers us to say "no" to pagan cultural and legal pressures. As citizens of an eternal city, we cannot drift along with the secular streams, acting as if this world is all that matters. We have a higher allegiance; we take our orders from the Heavenly King. We will bow to no earthly authority if it conflicts with our God-given responsibilities. We report to heaven, not to Earth.

After Martin Niemöller came out courageously opposing Hitler's agenda, his fellow pastors strongly condemned him, saying they thought that sensitive political matters could be handled more diplomatically. He replied, "What does it matter how we look in Germany compared with how we look in heaven?"[3]

A good question. So, how does the church of Jesus Christ look in heaven?

We can learn from Augustine, but the Apostle Paul gives us the actual Word of God.

THE CHURCH: THE CITY OF GOD

Thankfully, the Bible has examples showing us how we are to live in the midst of a pagan culture. Virtually every letter in the New Testament was written to a church that was an island of righteousness in a sea of pagan values. Repeatedly we are exhorted to maintain our purity and not compromise with the political and moral pressures of our age. When we find ourselves as a minority in a majority pagan culture, we can take heart if we remember that eternity is what really counts.

Take, for example, the fact that Paul wrote the book of Philippians from a jail cell in Rome. It is a letter of optimism written from a city filled with hostility and violence. Who was ruling in Rome? Nero.

There was not a single Christian on the Roman Senate. There was no Christian political lobby, no watchdog committee to make sure that the interests of the Christians were being addressed. There were no courts where the false accusations could be justly resolved. Paul sat in a prison in Rome without due representation. The Christians were often falsely accused without having their own media gurus to set the record straight.

To readers who faced the hostility of their culture, Paul wrote, "our citizenship is in heaven" (Philippians 3:20). The Greek word is *politeuma,* from which we get our word, *politics.* He says that our citizenship, our *politics,* if you please, is in heaven.

Paul sketched the difference between the heavenly and earthly citizenship. He was both a citizen of Rome and a citizen of heaven. He recognized that these two cities had two different values, two different loves, and two different lifestyles. It was because Augustine understood Paul that he would write that these two cities, "were created by two loves: the earthly city by self-love reaching the point of contempt for God, the heavenly city by the love of God reaching the point of contempt for self."[4]

Paul referred to those who were deceived, thinking themselves as friends of the cross but in reality were its enemies. "For many, of whom I have often told you and now tell you even with tears, walk as enemies of the cross of Christ. Their end is destruction, their god is their belly, and they glory in their shame, with minds set on earthly things. But our citizenship is in heaven, and from it we await a Savior, the Lord Jesus Christ, who will transform our lowly body to be like his glorious body, by the power that enables him even to subject all things to himself" (Philippians 3:18–21).

Paul wept when he described the contrast between true Christians and the imposters who claimed to be friends of the cross but denied it by their lives and theology. He warned that not everyone who says they are Christians are real followers of Christ. They belong to the city of man though they profess to belong to the city of God.

As already noted above, Paul describes the imposters in explicit terms: "Their end is destruction, their god is their belly, and they glory in their shame, with minds set on earthly things" (v. 19). For many people, their god is their appetite, either by taking pride in their diet, or by choosing to overeat, or fulfilling every craving of the flesh including alcoholism, drugs, and sensuality of every kind. They glory in that which should give them shame.

Contemporary man is convinced he can heal his own soul if only he will be open, "honest," and "authentic." A man who "comes out of the closet" is honored despite the fact that he leaves his wife and children to survive on their own while he pursues life with another man. Thus, the most shameful thing is revealed without a twinge of shame. Pity them as they try to purify their own souls by the dirty water from within! Light is proclaimed as darkness; darkness is proclaimed as light. The citizens of the city of man invite deception; they are motivated by a willing blindness.

Citizens of the city of God have food to eat of which the world knows nothing. They know that one shall not live by bread alone, but by every word that proceeds out of the mouth of God. They are learning to be content with God. And they agree with the person who said, "He who has God and everything else has no more than he who has God only."[5]

The citizens of the city of God speak a different language—a speech which betrays them. They speak with the recognizable accent of heaven. They may be disappointed when their treasures on Earth are stolen, but they are not dismayed. They know the difference between the temporary and the permanent, between the seen and the unseen. They rejoice in that which cannot be taken from them.

In contrast, the citizens of the earthly kingdom pin all of their hopes on the news that comes to them from Earth. They long for the assurance of more wealth, power, and sexual freedom. They believe that "you only live once," therefore they must "go for the gusto." Their desires are aroused by the latest pleasure, the lure of wealth, and the quest for power.

Citizens of heaven look for their Heavenly King. They "await a Savior, the Lord Jesus Christ, who will transform our lowly body to be like his glorious body" (Philippians 3:20–21). They look for Him because they love Him and are eager to "see Him as He is."

Two different cities.

Different values, different citizens, and different futures.

Thus, as Augustine said, we must separate ourselves from the values of the world without abandoning the world. If we say we are followers of the cross, we must live what we profess. We must always live with a higher allegiance.

DUAL CITIZENSHIP

Where does all of this leave us here in America?

By all accounts, we have lost the culture war. Abortion on demand, same-sex marriage, transgenderism forced upon our school children—all of this and more has fragmented the United States of America. We no longer have shared core values, we are divided racially, culturally, and politically. What do we do? How do we navigate dual citizenship?

We must not pretend that we are still a majority that can win the culture back to respect for the Constitution, the rule of law, and a shared "Judeo-Christian consensus." We are "strangers and pilgrims" on the earth as Peter told his readers (see 1 Peter 2:11, KJV. See also Hebrews 11:13).

We must be involved at all levels of society, but with a distinctly biblical agenda. Jesus warned that in the last days there would be wars, betrayals, apostasy, iniquity, and violence. And Paul expanded with his own list of sins (2 Timothy 3:1–3). The simple fact is that all of society will never be transformed; the consequences of our fallen humanity will always be with us. The church will always be a minority in a culture, a powerful minority to be sure, but a minority nevertheless. We cannot pretend that our battles can be won by casual Christians who think that going to church on Sunday and giving some money fulfills their obligations.

There are no easy answers.

We begin by strengthening our churches. We must return to those truths that made the church great. We must proclaim a message that is nothing less than the direct intervention of God in our world. Yes, we must fight, but we must fight like Christ who never wavered from His message of spiritual redemption in the midst of depressing political and social abuses.

We need pastors who will help guide the flock in navigating the cultural pressures that are constantly bombarding the faithful. A host of questions must be answered: How do we witness in the workplace? How should we approach "gender sensitivity" training? How do we help our children process the godless sexual curriculum in the public schools?

These are not simple questions, and there is not a one-size-fits-all answer. We must call on God to give us the wisdom we all need. We need to know what to do and have the courage to do it. We must refuse to be contaminated by the world's appetites.

We must also be willing to accept the consequences of our obedience to Christ. The early church did not complain about being imprisoned, falsely accused, or even beaten for the cause of Christ. Paul wrote, "When reviled, we bless; when persecuted, we endure; when slandered, we entreat. We have become, and are still, like the scum of the world, the refuse of all things" (1 Corinthians 4:12–13).

When confronted by the pleasures of the world, we choose the pleasures of God. We guard our hearts and minds even as we discharge our earthly citizenship. When shouted down, we reply with compassion; when told that we are bigots, we respond with reason and civility. When confronted with false doctrine, we take our stand with biblical truth.

We refuse to be shamed into silence.

HE WHO DOES THE WILL OF GOD
ABIDES FOREVER

Having had the privilege of being the senior pastor of The Moody Church for 36 years, you can imagine that I have been greatly impacted by the life and ministry of its founder, D.L. Moody. I have visited his grave in Northfield, Massachusetts, numerous times, and 120 years after his death, you can still read the words of his favorite text etched in the granite.

He who does the will of God abides forever.

Moody knew that his first obligation was to do the will of God; his loyalty was the city of God, not the city of man. On the cross, Jesus purchased our salvation. Those of us who believe now have the responsibility of carrying our cross into the world. And if we do His will, we will abide forever.

Augustine, upon hearing his beloved Rome had been trashed reportedly said, "Whatever men build, men will destroy. So let's get on with building the Kingdom of God."

The citizens of heaven must return to doing what only the citizens of heaven can do. We must keep pointing beyond this life to the next and encourage others to join us on our pilgrimage to the eternal City of God.

And we must count the cost.

Footnotes

1. Sack of Rome (410), https://en.wikipedia.org/wiki/Sack_of_Rome_(410)
2. Saint Augustine, *The City of God* (New York: Image Books, 1958), 309.
3. Chuck Colson, *Kingdoms in Conflict* (Grand Rapids: Zondervan 1989), 146.
4. Eleonore Stump and Norman Kretzmann, eds., *The Cambridge Companion to Augustine* (Cambridge University Press, 2001), 217.
5. Quoted in C.S. Lewis, *The Weight of Glory* (New York: HarperOne, 2015), 34.

CHAPTER TWO

THE CROSS, THE FLAG, AND THE UNRAVELING OF AMERICA

I already respected the American flag when I entered the United States as a Canadian back in 1970, long before I became a U.S. citizen. I can say honestly that despite the many faults of the United States—and there are many—I am unashamedly proud to be an American; I gladly say the Pledge of Allegiance and love "Old Glory."

The words in the Pledge, "the Flag of the United States of America," were intended to make clear to immigrants that this was not the flag of their home country, but a flag intended to represent the new country to which they now belonged. President Dwight D. Eisenhower added the words, "under God" so that "from this day forward, the millions of our school children will daily proclaim in every city and town, every village and rural school house, the dedication of our nation and our people to the Almighty....in this way we shall constantly strengthen those spiritual weapons which forever will be our country's most powerful resource, in peace or in war."[1] Despite our diversity of religion, race, and status, the flag and our Pledge of Allegiance and what it represents, was to give us the political cohesion to be "one nation under God."

But that cohesion is broken. Athletes disrespect the flag by refusing to stand for the national anthem, atheists object to the words "under God," and a Muslim woman refused to say the Pledge calling it an instrument of "forced assimilation." Some activists are saying that the Pledge represents America's dark history of "white supremacy." A few years ago, a pastor here in Chicago, Bishop James Dukes, asked the mayor to tear down the monument of George Washington mounted on a horse in Washington Park (so named after our first president) because he had slaves. We are seeing what one writer calls, "a nationwide temper tantrum." Nothing good is expected to come about by these actions that only fuel raw anger and hatred on both sides.

If you feel tension between your loyalty to the state and your loyalty to God, you are not alone. Christians have always struggled with their loyalty to the laws of their country and their loyalty to God. By no means did they think it always necessary to obey their government. Whether it was the midwives who disobeyed Pharaoh's orders to kill the Jewish babies, or the Apostles who said they would obey God rather than man, Christians have always had an allegiance to their heavenly citizenship that trumped earthly kings and flags. We should always be wary of a blind nationalism that says, "My country, right or wrong!"

In America, most Christians have gladly recited the Pledge of Allegiance because the laws of the United States have, for the most part, been in line with core Christian values. But there is no doubt that a day is coming when faithful Christians will have to be lawbreakers to be loyal to Jesus Christ. Already some have done just that and paid a heavy price.

But—and this is my concern—our present toxic political, moral, and racial environment has stirred seething tensions that are tearing us apart. The idea of a nation held together by one language, one common core of beliefs, and a unified immigration policy is passing us by.

But before we go any further into this controversial subject, let us take a step back and ask: What is the relationship Christians should have with the state? And what is the relationship between Christians and the flag?

Thankfully, Jesus speaks to these issues.

JESUS, CAESAR, AND THE CHURCH

In order to entrap Him, Christ's enemies posed a question, "Teacher, we know that you are true and teach the way of God truthfully, and you do not care about anyone's opinion, for you are not swayed by appearances.

Tell us, then, what you think. Is it lawful to pay taxes to Caesar, or not?" (Matthew 22:16–17).

Remember that the Romans occupied the land, exacting exorbitant taxes and gloating in their greed. The Jews had no alternative but to pay what was demanded. Needless to say, the Romans and their taxes were despised.

If Christ said, "Yes, pay these taxes," He would be on the wrong side of popular opinion. You couldn't find a Jew who said it was good and right to pay taxes to these foreigners, these idolaters. They paid taxes only because they *had* to.

If Christ said, "No, do not pay taxes to Caesar," they might turn Him over to the Roman authorities. To speak openly against Rome was a crime that would not go unpunished. Christ, however, countered their question with a request.

"Show Me the coin for the tax."

After they give him a coin, He asks them, "Whose likeness and inscription is this?"

"Caesar's."

The Jews hated the sight of a Roman denarius, not only because it reminded them of their slavery, but because the image on the coin was idolatrous. In the minds of the pagans, Caesar was a god. Thus, the Jews were forced to support state-sponsored idolatrous worship.

"Therefore render to Caesar the things that are Caesar's,

and to God the things that are God's," Christ replied.

In other words, *yes,* they should pay taxes to Caesar even though Caesar would use the money to pay Roman soldiers to maintain a stranglehold on the Jewish nation, but even so, *taxes were to be paid.* They were to be subject to the powers that be, however unjust. But—and this is important—the people were also to *pay to God the allegiance they owed Him.* No one had ever said this before with such clarity.

Christ taught we have an obligation to pay our dues to a corrupt pagan political regime and at the same time pay our dues to God. As believers it is possible to discharge our obligations to the city of God as well as to the city of man. The spheres overlap and yet are separate.

KINGDOMS IN CONFLICT

Christians in the early Roman Empire believed that they could still be good citizens of Rome even though they worshiped the One True and Living God. But Caesar disagreed. To be a good Roman, the authorities insisted, you had to accept the Roman religion. And for those who were not willing to affirm that "Caesar was lord," the lions were waiting.

Of course, when the tables were turned and Rome was "Christianized," there was still no freedom of religion within the empire. Heretics were burned at the stake, killed with the sword, or drowned. Often the first victims were those genuine Christians who refused to synthesize their faith with prevailing pagan ideas. Small groups who rejected the inherent validity of the sacraments, and as a matter of conscience, believed in adult baptism, were routinely persecuted.

For example, in AD 400, the Donatists separated from the church, insisting on adult baptism and the belief that a priest had to live a moral life in order for the sacraments to convey grace to the worshippers. These congregations were hunted down, persecuted and killed, wiped off the face of the earth. The "true" Christians were in charge and they were determined to run things according to their laws.

As the Catholic Church became powerful, political appointments were sold to the highest bidder and indulgences were used to fill the church coffers. The doctrinal deviations were so twisted and the political deals so corrupt that Martin Luther chose to break from the Catholic Church and, as best he could, return to the faith of the New Testament.

With the coming of the Reformation, conversion was now individualized; personal faith in Christ was proclaimed as necessary for salvation. Neither one's parents nor a priest could make an infant (or an adult for that matter), a Christian. The Reformers knew that no one could be forced to believe for unless God changes the heart of the individual, there can be no lasting transformation.

When Luther declared "My conscience is captive to the Word of God. I cannot and I will not recant..."[2] he was enunciating a principle that would later lead to freedom of religion: no one can coerce another to believe, thus individual consciences must be respected. Freedom of religion did not immediately follow the Reformation, but it was on its way.

However, Europe did not have complete freedom of religion until the Peace of Westphalia in 1648. The seeds of the Reformation gave birth to religious liberty.

For the better part of twenty centuries, the conflict between church and state, freedom and religious tyranny, dominated the history of Western Europe. Religious freedom is a precious gift and too often it is taken for granted.

FREEDOM IN AMERICA

When the pilgrims came to America, it was to establish freedom of religion, but not for everyone. Roger Williams was banished from New England because he was a Baptist. The Puritans, who followed the covenant theology of Calvin, came seeking freedom for the Protestant faith. They would have been scandalized by the idea of religious freedom as we think of it today.

However, by the time the Bill of Rights was ratified in 1791, the participants believed that doctrinal agreement was not necessary for the preservation of the union. Of special interest to us is the First Amendment with its famous phrase, "Congress shall make no law respecting an establishment of religion, or prohibiting the free exercise thereof."

The intention of this phrase was to limit the power of government; to make sure that the United States did not establish a state church to which all must adhere. Also, the government was not to interfere with religious expression. And most assuredly, it was believed that religion could and should be practiced in the political sphere. Just witness the verses of Scripture engraved in government buildings in Washington, D.C. I will not enter into a debate as to whether America was founded as a Christian nation, however, there is no doubt that it was founded on what we call "Judeo-Christian values."

The notion that there is a "wall of separation" that allows a rock concert but forbids the singing of hymns in the same park, is a construct that the radical left uses to try to silence the voice of Christians. The idea that a child drawing a picture of the nativity scene on a school chalkboard constitutes government sanction of religion is, of course, absurd. But a secular state will always be hostile to religion and seek to limit its influence. Absurdity has never deterred the radical left from pursuing its agenda.

Where did the idea of religious freedom come from? Most of our textbooks trace it back to the eighteenth-century Enlightenment when advances in science and communication changed the Western world. However, as we have already noted, the seeds of freedom were planted in the Protestant Reformation with its emphasis on individual conversion and the freedom of conscience.

Is it possible to believe in any religion you might choose (or no religion at all) and still be a good American citizen? Can you honor the flag even if you don't believe in God? The Founding Fathers answered this question by saying *yes* and *no*. They would not force anyone to be religious, but they also believed that religion was "an indispensable support" to freedom. Yes, an atheist can still be a bona fide American citizen. But the Founding Fathers believed that the populace could not maintain such magnificent freedoms without the underpinnings of religion. Freedom, they believed, would be so abused by the irreligious that the nation would eventually rot. Without widespread belief in transcendent values, freedom would turn into anarchy, morality into personal self-interest.

The indispensable support is eroding daily. Opinion polls show that most Americans believe in God, but many live as atheists, paying little attention to the Bible as God's revelation. The proliferation of New Age thought, the radical individualism that clamors for personal rights, and the influx of refugees who maintain their primary loyalty to their countries of origin, tears at the very fabric of our families and institutions.

Humanism is now coming to its logical conclusion in education, law, and morality. The result is as bad as the Founding Fathers imagined it might be.

What shall we do?

When we are angry it's possible to do the wrong thing. Our first inclination is to lash out, insisting it's time to "take this country back." Unfortunately, such a mentality betrays the fact that we probably don't understand how we got here in the first place.

As pointed out in the previous chapter, we are not in a cultural war, we are in a spiritual conflict. We must fight in God's way and with God's weapons. We must understand the proper relationship between the cross and the flag, between God and Caesar. We must be able to distinguish the Christian dream from the American dream. We must learn from history the dangers of giving first allegiance to the flag.

Should Christians be patriotic?

That depends, of course, on the core values of the country to which you belong. No doubt the core Judeo-Christian values of our culture in the United States have fragmented. Anger, outrage, and a destructive emphasis on racial diversity are polarizing our culture. Disagreements about immigration and political priorities bombard the news. Civility, reason, and genuine debate has given way to accusations and name calling. This is certainly not the America we once knew.

The terrain of this chapter is fraught with mine fields. Thanks to our nationalistic instincts, it's difficult for us to look at our nation objectively. It's hard for us to face the fact that we as a church might be veering off track, losing sight of our most important goal. It's difficult to admit that we just might have mistaken the American dream for God's dream.

Come with me on a tour of Scripture and history as we search for firm ground upon which we can stand to unravel the entanglements between church and state, God and country, the cross and the flag.

THE FLAG ABOVE THE CROSS

"My country right or wrong!"

In a Berlin museum I saw pictures of the swastika with the cross of Christ in the center. As I gazed upon that spectacle, I decided to study the history of the German church under Hitler to try to find out why it had embraced his agenda. The stage had been set in World War I when young men dying on the battlefield were depicted as martyrs for Christ, and the people were convinced that a strong Germany meant a strong church. In my book, *Hitler's Cross,* I explain how this confusion of crosses (the swastika and cross of Christ) led to widespread support of Hitler when he arrived on the scene. But the churches at the time were quite oblivious to the fact that they had traded their biblical faith for the civil religion of Germany, a form of Christianity that called for a powerful defense, a strong economy, and unquestioned patriotism. They were seduced by a subtle confusion of kingdoms.

Christians have always been in danger of rendering to Caesar that which is God's. We can subtly become nationalistic, affirming that because our country is great, it must also be right and good. It's always easier to see the weaknesses of another country than it is to see our own. For us, it's hard to determine where the flag ends and the cross begins.

Certainly, God has blessed the United States because of its Christian heritage. But we do harm to the body of Christ when we cannot clearly distinguish between the cross and the flag. If we confuse the two, it will be to the detriment and weakness of the church.

Today, some Christian leaders long for a return to a basic civil religion where everyone marches in line with minimal religious convictions. Civil religion has some benefits because it provides a national context that is conducive to true Christianity. But it should never be confused with biblical Christianity. As G.K. Chesterton is to have said: A coziness between church and state may good for the state, but bad for the church.

What is civil religion? Henry Steele Commager, one of America's leading historians, defines it, "the new nation began with two religions, one secular and one spiritual. Almost all Americans acknowledged themselves as Christians, [but] they generally shared what has been called 'a civil religion'...a secular faith in America herself, in democracy, equality and freedom which were equated with America in the American mission and the American destiny."[3] It's been said that the substance of this civil religion tends to push God to the "outer fringes," calling on Him for state functions but not allowing Him to be involved in our day-to-day thinking or operation of normal life.

We must remember that civil religion, however desirable is not true Christianity.

In his book, *Cease Fire: Searching for Sanity in America's Culture Wars*, Tom Sine reminds us that civil religion and Christianity are two very different faiths, bowing to two very different deities, following two very different agendas. Civil religion pushes the advancement of the United States through their nationalistic agenda, whereas the Christian faith is committed to advancing God's transnational kingdom.

Dietrich Bonhoeffer warned the church in Germany that it was bowing before the wrong altar. The pride of the church, he said, must be rebuked by the humiliation of the cross:

God's verdict means our defeat, it means our humiliation, it means God's mocking anger at all human arrogance, being puffed up, trying to be important in our own right. It means the cross above the world…The Cross of Christ, means the bitter scorn of God for all human heights, bitter suffering… with Gideon we kneel before the altar and say 'Lord on the Cross, be Thou alone our Lord. Amen.'[4]

Lord on the Cross be Thou alone our Lord. Amen!

I personally want the Unit;ed States to remain strong, to have a strong national defense, and to maintain our freedoms. I want our congressmen and congresswomen to continue to swear allegiance to the Constitution with a hand on the Bible and not the Qur'an. America has supported mission agencies around the world and has fought wars that brought freedom to countries. I have been to Normandy and visited the American cemetery with its 9,000 white crosses. I am glad to live in a country that is the envy of the world. However, being consumed with corruption in government, the wasting of our taxes, the national debt, and funding of the abortion providers, and whether we should have open borders can be a danger for Christians because we're getting angry for the wrong reasons. Sometimes we are angry, not because Christ is daily dishonored and the true God not worshipped, but because we fear that our taxes and family values are not being protected. Our creature comforts are the issues that really stir our ire.

On Christmas day, says Tom Sine, we want our living rooms to look as if there was an explosion in a department store! Yes, extravagance is the American way. But is it the Christian way? Several years ago, just before Christmas, I visited the country of Belarus which had just gained independence from communist control. I asked my friend Victor Krutko what the stores carried for the holidays. He looked at me with a wry smile and said, "There is no Christmas shopping; the Christians just sing hymns, but there are no presents, the stores are empty, the people have no money." Are they less Christian than the rest of us? I think not.

I'm convinced that many angry Christians would be pacified if only we could return this country to the 1950s when there were fewer illicit drugs, pornography was only sold on the black market, and movies, for the most part, portrayed family values. They would be satisfied with this change even if no one were converted to Christ in the process! I do understand how it might be more conducive to raise children in such an environment. But many Christians would be content if Christ were accepted as lawgiver to restore order to society, even if He were not accepted as Savior to *rescue* society.

The late Edward Dobson, who at one time was a member of the Moral Majority, changed his mind about the power of politics. He writes, "Politics cannot offer permanent solutions because it is based on a flawed view of sin and society. One of its premises is that if you elect the 'right' representatives who will pass the 'right' legislation you will have the 'right' society. But we know this is not true."[5] We have forgotten that the reason the world will never share our values is because the world does not share our Christ.

The cross must always stand alone, unopposed by competing loyalties. Its message must never be sacrificed on the altar of our own political or social agenda or by whichever political party holds office. Of course, political policy has an effect on our lives, but right laws cannot make people good, nor can they make godly families. Our message must be more profound than any government policy could possibly be. It is a message that must penetrate the very depths of the human heart.

THE CROSS ABOVE THE FLAG

How then do we discharge the dual obligations to which Christ referred? How do we pay our dues to the city of God and to the city of man? To God and to Caesar? To fulfill our duty to Caesar, we are to pray for those who have the rule over us, we are to pay taxes, and we are, as far as our conscience allows, to support government policy.

To fulfill our duty to God we realize that we must love the Lord with all our heart, soul, mind, and strength (Mark 12:30). We must return to the gospel of our forefathers, the supernatural God of the apostles and their followers. Our responsibility in the world is to showcase Christ, to put Him on display so that the world can see what He is able to do in the lives of those who trust Him. We are to show His worthiness and invite others to believe in Him.

Our responsibility is not to show the world that we can win playing its own political game. It is not to prove to the world that we can shout as loudly as they can when our rights are violated. It is not our responsibility to warn them that they had better follow our morality because we will soon be "taking our country back."

We have a message that must be heard above the din of political posturing and rancor. We have an agenda that is even more important than saving the United States, it is holding the cross high so that God might be pleased to save Americans.

How do we fulfill our duties as citizens of Earth as well as citizens in heaven?

First, *we must choose the right battle.* Is our real conflict cultural, moral, or political? Actually, it's none of those. Our real conflict is doctrinal and spiritual. We can argue that Christian morality is better, we can try to clean up our culture by legislation and boycotts, but our efforts will be like trying to mop up the floor with the faucet still running and the sink overflowing. We are trying to convince citizens of Earth to live as though they are citizens of heaven. But they're not buying what we are selling.

Why should we convince the unconverted to pray in public schools? How can we expect them to pray to a God whom they neither know nor love? Our responsibility is not to put prayer back in our public schools but, as Jim Cymbala has said, to put it back in our churches and homes. Remember, God's agenda is the conversion of the heart not merely the convincing of the mind.

When Paul entered the pagan city of Corinth, he didn't begin a campaign to clean up the city's morals. He preached Christ crucified, urging people to flee from the city of man to the city of God. Of course, Christians should be fighting pornography, gambling, and other moral sins that plague our society, but our first duty is to cleanse the church of these sins. Only then can we prepare to spread our influence beyond our walls.

We can even appeal to common grace and enlist the help of the those of other religions in trying to shore up support for our agenda. But let us not confuse such a moralistic campaign with the essence of Christianity. Christianity, properly understood, is a message that a Holy

God punishes sin, and if we do not flee to the protection of Christ, we will be damned forever.

Have we forgotten that if there is any good news in America it will not come from Washington, D.C., but through the lips of God's people? We cannot evangelize America unless every Christian begins to witness for Christ wherever God has planted them.

Second, *we must use the right weapons.* In the United States, millions of Christians belong to one or more political organizations that are dedicated to "the Christian agenda." Politics in America is based on a majority vote and since Christians are a minority, what can we do when we are out-financed and out-voted?

We are grateful when Catholics, Jews, and Mormons, etc. stand with us against some of the destructive moral evils we have to face such as abortion, gambling, homosexual values, and the like. But please hear me when I say that *issues which have such widespread support cannot possibility be the primary mission of the church.*

The doctrine of the exclusivity of Christ who purchased our justification unites us as believers, but it also means that we cannot pretend that those who join us on our moral battles are truly "one" with us. As has been said, it is better to be divided by truth than united by error. Luther was right when he said justification by faith is the doctrine by which the church stands or falls. We are handing the keys to the traitors if we think that we can compromise the one message that can save us in exchange for greater cooperation on moral and political issues.

I'm not saying that we should withdraw from legal battles, particularly those that have to do with freedom of religion. Organizations such as the Rutherford Institute and the Alliance Defending Freedom have successfully challenged violations of First Amendment religious privileges. However, we must be realistic and realize that as the steamroller of secularism gains increasing momentum, even these victories might be short lived. The simple fact is that throughout the 2,000 years of church history, the church has seldom had freedom of religion. Read the history of the church in Europe, Russia, and China and you will be convinced that *it is not necessary to have freedom in order to be faithful.*

I am neither arguing for passivity or isolation. Christians have been on the forefront of legislation to pass child labor laws and abolish slavery. We should be in the forefront to protect unborn children from the abortionist's knife. But even here we need to be reminded that a change in the law does not bring about a change in the heart. People will not share our values until they share our Christ.

We must use persuasion for our point of view rather than attack-dog political confrontation. Let us appeal to compassion and justice, but not draw lines in the sand that force even moderate people to take sides. Thanks to what theologians call common grace, we might find support from many people who are not specifically Christian. This is, in my opinion, the proper use of what Francis Schaeffer used to call "co-belligerency."

And if we want to lobby for other matters like a balanced budget amendment or tax breaks for families or even support for the NRA, if we wish to do this, we should, but let us not nail these agendas to the cross as if they are the "Christian" agenda. I grieve because, for many observers, *the cross of Christ appears to the world as a dilapidated bulletin board cluttered with a whole host of issues!*

We have to intentionally rectify our reputation which has been tarnished by the radicals among us. We can only win America if every single Christian becomes involved, assuming the delicate task of taking a firm and loving stand on the issues yet presenting spiritual healing to a society that is afflicted with the disease called sin. We are to hold up the cross and display "the excellencies of him who called you out of darkness into his marvelous light" (1 Peter 2:9).

PERSONAL WITNESSING

The average person will never be convinced of the credibility of the cross until they become personally acquainted with someone who lives out the Christian faith, applying its implications to every situation, even at great personal cost. Many Americans have never met someone who is pro-life yet also loves the women who have had abortions. They think they have never met anyone who is opposed to the homosexual agenda yet loves homosexuals. They do not know someone who is opposed to sex education of young kids and yet is willing to work with the school board to find an alternative. I believe that there are tens of thousands of Christians who have the right perspective, but they have been reduced to silence by the loud din of the progressive activists with a compliant media as it smothers us with pro-abortion, pro-homosexual, and pro-trans rhetoric. Speak we must, but that isn't enough.

We must bring the cross out of our churches and carry it to a hurting world. Our task is not to save Ameria, but to save Americans by living the gospel. "Keep your conduct among the Gentiles honorable, so that when they speak against you as evildoers, they may see your good deeds and glorify God on the day of visitation" (1 Peter 2:12).

Several times I have stood in the "Luther Stube" in the Wartburg Castle where it is said Luther threw an inkwell at the devil (enterprising tour leaders used to put soot on the wall so as not to disappoint tourists). But an inkwell thrown at the devil would hardly do the fiend harm; you cannot fight against a spirit with a material weapon.

Perhaps there is a better explanation of what happened in that room. In his *Table Talks,* Luther said that he "fought the devil with ink." Very probably he meant that he fought the devil through the translation of the New Testament into German, a feat accomplished in that small room in just eleven weeks! What an inkwell thrown at the devil could never accomplish, the Word of God did!

We are constantly in danger of using the wrong weapons because we have incorrectly identified the enemy. Our greatest weapon is not politics, important though that is, but the blessed news of the gospel, accurately proclaimed. If we are not careful, we will expect ink wells to do what only God's Word can do!

Politics is a game of high risk. If you live by the ballot box, you must die by the ballot box. It is a game of numbers where the majority rules, whether the majority is right or wrong. The question is how we shall live in a culture in which we are outnumbered, even with our coalitions and voting blocs.

We must *fight with the right attitude.* Of course we must speak up on behalf of preborn infants. Of course we must work together to end racism and bring about just laws. But we must fight with an attitude of humility. We should not approach society as if we have all the answers for the escalation of violence and child abuse. We should not pretend that if we were in charge, then America's moral toboggan slide would end.

We engage society, not to lord it over others, not to

self-righteously point out their sins. We serve, knowing the sins that exist in the world are also found in the church. We have no illusions that the city of man can become sanctified. We pray for the city of man as Abraham did for Sodom and Gomorrah, knowing that we have relatives who live within its gates. We should be the first to help the single mother who does not know how she can cope with her baby. We reach out to those who struggle with same-sex attraction, not with self-righteous condemnation, but with the recognition that we are also sinners who could easily be a part of that lifestyle. We always judge ourselves more harshly than we judge others.

We do not take the cross which should humble us and turn it into a club to make the world "shape up." We pursue our primary mission with single-mindedness and heartfelt conviction. We exercise our freedom to vote but we also know that the United States cannot be restored by a change of administrations, even if there were such a thing as a "Christian" party. But if Luther could not vanquish the devil by throwing an inkwell at him, neither can we vanquish our foe by the ballot box or the courts.

We have a powerful weapon if only we would use it.

THE CROSS AGAINST THE FLAG

How do we deal with matters of conscience?

The government to whom the early Christians paid

taxes made demands the Christians couldn't accept. When the state required them to confess Caesar as lord, the Christians had to say *no* to Caesar in order to say *yes* to God. And when the state forbad them to preach the gospel, they affirmed that they had to *"obey God rather than men."*

When do we disobey? The answer, of course, is when we are told to do something that the Bible forbids or when we're asked to refrain from doing what the Bible commands. If you lived in East Germany in the 1960s and you were asked to help build the Berlin Wall, you built it. But if you were told that you couldn't share the gospel with those working alongside of you, you couldn't abide by that restriction. You shared the gospel carefully and wisely, but you shared it nevertheless. You are called to preach the gospel "to every creature."

What do you do if your children are expected to see steamy sex films in school as a part of the sex education curriculum? You go to the teacher and try to resolve the matter. If that doesn't work, you go to the school board and, if necessary, join a coalition of parents who are willing to protest this violation of parent/child responsibility. You do not antagonize others with strong words of condemnation or by demonizing those who don't see matters your way. You realize that by your life and attitude Christ is on display. But as someone has said, a Christian without courage is the same as a practical atheist.

What do we do when our churches are told they will lose their tax-exempt status if they refuse to marry homosexual couples? We can seek to block that legislation, arguing that the churches and other charitable organizations provide valuable services to the community. We do not call our opponents names, instead we hope that reason will prevail. Seek the advice of legal experts, but do not imply that the church which is built upon Christ will wither away if tax exemption were denied.

We must disagree *wisely*. Our speech is always to be "seasoned with grace." If a child is forbidden to draw a nativity scene in school, we do not call the "Center of Truth and Justice." We talk to the teacher, to school administrators. We try to work with those who belong to the city of man, rather than generating needless antagonism.

In a time of shrill voices, the church must keep its cool and be a calming voice of reason and broad political acceptance without being co-opted by one side or another in these escalating disputes. We must continue to stand united at the foot of the cross and invite other sinners to join us regardless of their background, political party, or immigration status. The church is still America's best hope.

We must disagree *honestly*. We never misrepresent our adversaries in an appeal letter to our constituency so that we might stir people to give to our cause. Unfortunately, we all receive fundraising appeals that are sensational, overblown, and intended to make us angry (conventional wisdom says that only angry people send money). Equally foolish is the assumption that the organization that wants our funds is actually in a position to fix whatever has gone wrong!

We disagree *humbly*. We know we will be vilified if we stand our ground on a host of issues, but we don't retaliate with anger, fighting fire with fire. We should expect to be misrepresented in the media. We don't castigate the media as if our cause is dependent on their "fair reporting." Why argue with the *Washington Post* about how many attended a pro-life rally? If the paper said 200,000 and we think it is 500,000, so be it. Why should we expect those who are pro-choice to be fair in reporting on a matter about which they have such deeply held beliefs? Have we who are on the other side of this volatile issue always been "fair"?

Since many Christians often don't act "christianly" why should we expect fair and even-handed behavior from the unconverted? We should not be alarmed if unbelievers act like unbelievers; we should be alarmed, however, when believers act like *un*believers!

We should not see ourselves as the "persecuted minority," whining about how difficult the world has made it for us. We humbly acknowledge that unless God helps us, we will not be helped; unless we are redeemed in His grace, we shall be lost. We stand with sinners, acknowledging that apart from unmerited grace, we would be where they are today.

Take heart!

It is possible for the kingdom of man to decline and the kingdom of God to be doing quite well! In fact, the church has the responsibility of picking up the pieces of a rotting society. As everything that has ever been nailed down is torn up, we have the privilege of coming in the name of Christ to people in need.

Missionary experts tell us that the church in China, where vicious persecution has been felt for the past 50 years, has grown more than the church in Taiwan with its freedoms. I say this not to glorify persecution, but to simply point out that the success of the city of God is not dependent on the favor of city of man.

We are, after all, pilgrims en route to our permanent home.

Christ never promised it would be easy.

Footnotes

1. "God in the White House," PBS, https://www.pbs.org/wgbh/americanexperience/features/godinamerica-white-house/

2. Roland H. Bainton, *Here I Stand: A Life of Martin Luther* (Nashville, Abingdon Press, 2013), 182.

3. Henry Steele Commager, *Jefferson, Nationalism, and the Enlightenment* (New York: George Braziller Incorporated, 1975), 189–90.

4. Mary Bosanquet, *The Life and Death of Dietrich Bonhoeffer* (London: Hodder and Stoughton, 1968), 121–122.

5. Edward Dobson, "Taking Politics out of the Sanctuary" *Christianity Today,* May 20, 1996, https://www. christianitytoday.com/ct/1996/may20/6t6016.html

ERWIN W. LUTZER

CHAPTER THREE

POLITICS AND THE CROSS IN GOD'S HEART

Political wrangling in the United States is to be expected. Politicians debate, criticize, and argue. We listen, observe, then choose one side or the other about the issue at hand. And then we vote our conscience. Our leaders are far from perfect, but we make our decision not by choosing the perfect candidate but the best candidate from which we can select.

Where we come down politically has much to do with our view of human nature. If you believe that people are essentially good, you will find excuses for evil deeds outside of the person himself. If he steals, it's because he's poor; if he commits murder, it's because of his home life; if he does not succeed, he's a victim of society. I still remember back when Bobby Kennedy was assassinated, his wife said she didn't blame the shooter, but the culture that produced him.

The radical left stresses oppression, victimhood, and inequality as reasons for crime and poverty. Only the oppressors are seen as evil; the oppressed bear little or no responsibility for their plight. The oppressed are basically good, and if given a chance, would live moral and prosperous lives. Fomenting division is important to their vision of "transforming America."

Without denying that we are influenced by outside forces, the Bible locates the seat of even in our own hearts, not in our circumstances. The human heart can be the seat of goodness, or it can be the seat of unspeakable evil. And sometimes both co-exist exist in the same person. Alexander Solzhenitsyn, a Russian historian who lived through the horrors of communism, said the line between good and evil runs through every human heart. People do evil because the seeds of evil reside in every one of us.

The Bible's view of human depravity is critical in understanding the conflict between the gospel and politics in our struggle for the soul and future of America. This chapter speaks about the depth of human need and the eternality of God's purposes; we have to see the importance of God's intervention in our sin-filled world.

Understanding the cross is critical in understanding human nature and its great need. At the end of this chapter we will apply it to our political crisis.

THE CROSS AND ITS POWER

The gospel is "the power of God unto salvation" precisely

because it transforms the human heart. If we don't see the urgency of the transformation of lives, there's no long-term hope for America or, for that matter, any country of the world. More precisely, there is no hope for any individual on the planet.

What we need is the gospel.

We as evangelicals have been so deeply shaped by the spirit of our age that many don't realize that we've bowed to the gods of modernity. Preaching might be widespread in America, Christian book sales might be on the increase, and the media might be expanding religious programming, but is the gospel widespread in America? Perhaps not.

Just listen to many of the sermons preached in America and you'll find the themes of popular culture: a belief in the essential goodness of man and the goals of happiness, wealth, and health. You'll hear messages rife with stories of miracles based just as much on the power of the human mind as the power of God. You'll find a great emphasis on spirituality, personal fulfillment, and openness to other belief systems. Absent is an emphasis on the depravity of man, the holiness of God, and the urgent need to humble ourselves and approach God through Christ's sacrifice alone.

I am interested in the early church simply because of how the gospel impacted their culture. The apostles found themselves up against a social, political, and religious barrier they couldn't move. They had no political appointments, no judgeships, and no freedom to properly voice their frustrations.

And yet they turned the world upside down.

Listen to what Peter said to his antagonists after he had been released from a Jerusalem prison, "And there is salvation in no one else, for there is no other name under heaven given among men by which we must be saved" (Acts 4:12).

There is a lesson here for Americans. The bleak political world Peter and the apostles lived in didn't shake Peter's confidence in God nor the need to get the message out. There was joy in the face of persecution and political uncertainty. The apostles seemed blissfully oblivious to the barriers that surrounded them; they were convinced that the message Christ gave them could not be suppressed by the authorities of the day. Neither did they naively think that everyone would believe. The fact that Christ promised them persecution is reason enough to show they didn't think the preaching of the gospel would bring about some kind of Christian utopia.

As I've stated, I believe in political involvement. As Americans we have the freedom of elections, the freedom to lobby for our convictions, and we have the right to exert our influence. We should vote, we should lobby, and Christians should run for political office. We should pray for those who have the rule over us. In the United States, we have both the privilege and obligation of exercising the freedoms that come with our citizenship.

But—and this is the point of this chapter—like the apostles we must be passionate about the fact that God has entered our world and we, like them, have a message that could grip the heart of the most notorious sinner. This confidence allowed the apostles to have an impact on society that was much greater than their numbers alone might suggest. Faced with ridicule, ostracism, and persecution, they kept the main thing the main thing. Even if no one had believed, they would have continued to do God's work, leaving the results in His hands.

If the cross is at the heart of God's agenda, it most assuredly should be at the heart of ours as well. When I speak of the cross, I do not refer to a piece of wood upon which Christ died, but the death itself, and not just the death, but His resurrection and ascension.

Rev. John Stott said, "Before we can begin to see the cross as something done *for* us…we have to see it as something done *by* us."[1] Our sin put Jesus on that cross. Where is the greatest evidence of God's love seen? On the cross. Where is God's greatest judgment and wrath against sin most clearly seen? On the cross. Jesus bore the wrath that is due us. God would have never put His Son through horrid suffering if there had been a cheaper way to do it.

But Jesus absorbed what you and I should have received; in short, *He bore our hell.* And now that justice has been satisfied, Jesus is just and the Justifier of those who believe on Him (see Romans 3:26), which means God is free to operate on the basis of grace and save even the vilest of sinners.

The cross is the hinge on which the door of history swings; it is the hub that holds the spokes of God's purposes. The Old Testament prophets pointed toward it and the New Testament prophets proclaimed it. And, properly understood, it is even today, "the power of God unto salvation." When we "cling to that old rugged cross" as the old familiar song encourages us to do, this is not mere sentimentality. This is the heart of our message and the heart of our power to combat the encroaching darkness.

God has chosen this world to be the stage on which a drama would unfold. Here on this planet the issues of justice and injustice, truth and error, kindness and cruelty are fought. God and the devil are pitted against each other, and thankfully there is no doubt about the outcome. God is the scriptwriter and He supervises this cosmic play, making sure it will turn out as planned. And His script was written long ago.

Come with me on a journey into the mind of God; we will encounter some challenging ideas and when we are finished, we will see our own political/cultural conflicts in new light. Looked at from the panorama of eternity, we will be encouraged to stay on target.

We will see that politics is temporal; the message of the cross is eternal.

THE CROSS IN GOD'S HEART

How long has the cross been a part of God's plan?

After Adam and Eve sinned, God told the serpent, "I will put enmity between you and the woman, and between your offspring and her offspring; he shall bruise your head, and you shall bruise his heel" (Genesis 3:15). God promised He would take the initiative, "I will..."

He also predicted that the redemption of man would involve suffering, "enmity" would be the order of the day. And thankfully, the seed of the woman (Christ) would crush the head of the serpent.

When did this plan form in God's mind? Was He actually expecting, perhaps hoping, that Adam and Eve would obey His command so that they would live in perpetual bliss? Or was the redemption of the cross in His mind long before Eve was mesmerized by the beautiful fruit of the forbidden tree?

There are two possible answers.

The first is to say that the plan to redeem man became a part of God's agenda when our first parents stood amid the ruins of paradise. Then and there He graciously concluded that He would do something about their predicament.

God, some have taught, had high hopes for Adam and Eve, but they disappointed Him, so He had to come up with another plan. In fact, one evangelical pastor in a message titled, "God the Gambler," said that God gambled on His creation, betting that they would serve Him. When He lost the gamble and Adam and Eve sinned, He did what any gambler does, He upped the ante and bet His Son. This pastor actually read John 3:16 as, "For God so loved the world that He *bet* His only begotten son..."

For this minister, if we dare call him such, there were no guarantees; God had no assurance that anyone would believe on Christ after He died for sinners. After all, because of "free will" it was conceivable that no one believe on Christ. God could have lost the whole gamble!

According to this scenario, the death of Christ was God's response to an emergency He was hoping would not happen. We can be grateful that God came to clean up the mess, but He lost the gamble. Nothing about His plans were certain, except the fact that He is loving so He can be expected to do whatever He can to help us.

Should it be any wonder why a message like that, proclaimed from some pulpits today, is unable to save sinners?

Second, there are those who would say that the idea of the cross was agreed upon at some point before the foundation of the world. Since the Father loves the Son, He agreed to give Him a community of redeemed humanity. And God the Spirit would be agent by which this gift of redemption would be mediated to mankind. Thus, there was a point at which the covenant was ratified, agreed to, and sealed.

Several Scriptures teach that there was such an agreement. Paul wrote to Titus, "in hope of eternal life, which God, who never lies, promised before the ages began" (Titus 1:2). This promise made before the foundation of the world was an agreement made by the members of the Trinity. Christ repeatedly referred to the elect as *"those whom the Father has given me."* They are the ones who are a part of the eternal plan of redemption.

This view is, of course, an immeasurably improved understanding of the cross in God's eternal purpose. God's dignity and sovereignty is restored to its rightful place in the story of redemption. Let's linger here for a moment.

So, to put it more clearly, I believe that the cross was always in the mind of God, even from the distant ages of eternity. The plan of redemption is as eternal as God. It makes no more sense to ask, "When did the idea of the cross have its beginning?" as it would be to ask, "When did God have a beginning?" As long as there was God, there was the cross in His heart.

There are two reasons I believe this.

First, God never learns anything. In fact, we can say that all of His decisions were already known to Him as long as He has existed, which is forever. We should never think that at any time God didn't quite know what to do and had to wrestle with the problem; that He looked at several options and made up His mind about what to do. As a friend of mine used to ask, "Has it ever dawned on you that nothing has ever dawned on God?"

Although all of God's works were known to Him from all of eternity, the cross was the focal point of His program. In redemption, His attributes would be most clearly displayed.

Second, if you still doubt that the cross is as eternal as God, hear the words of Paul, "[God] who saved us and called us to a holy calling, not because of our works but because of his own purpose and grace, which he gave us in Christ Jesus before the ages began" (2 Timothy 1:9). Literally, the Greek text reads that grace was granted to us "before the ages of eternity"!

We must pause to catch our breath. I, for one, cannot understand how God can have eternally existed; I more easily grasp the idea of eternity future, but not God's existence in eternity past. As the saying goes, we can't "get our mind around" such a concept. Yet, however much we struggle with the fact that God had no beginning, we can rejoice that the redeemed have been known to Him as long as He has existed! Already back then, it was certain that they would be granted grace. To put it differently, if you are redeemed, there never was a time when you were not already loved by God; there never was a time when you were not the object of His specific purpose. This is why John could say that our names were written in the Lamb's book of life "before the foundation of the world" (Revelation 13:8).

When Paul wrote that we are "chosen in Christ from before the foundation of the world" (Ephesians 1:4), we are evidently not to think that there was a specific point before creation that we were chosen; rather, the choice was as eternal as God. We were chosen, yes, but the choice existed as long as God has existed. Given the difficulty of comprehending eternity past, it is quite understandable that we speak of God as choosing, willing, and planning at some point before creation. We struggle with the idea that the script God wrote for the universe has existed as long as He has. What is important is that we realize that there was a cross in God's heart long before there was a cross that existed on Calvary. No gamble here.

If you are troubled, wondering whether you are among this chosen company, keep in mind that we can find out whether we are among "the elect." All we must do is come to Christ, transferring our trust to Him alone. When we do that, it is proof we are included in the number of the redeemed, those to whom grace has been shown "from all eternity." Indeed, the invitation is to "whosoever will."

God wants to be known by His creation as a redeeming God. To accomplish this, the scripted drama had to become a reality on Earth. It is unthinkable that His eternal plan would fail. Remember, the real story is God's redemptive history, not the fluctuating ebb and flow of the kingdoms of this world.

THE CROSS IN HISTORY

Since God's plan called for Christ's death, how was this to be brought about?

A coalition of God's enemies would conspire together to put Christ to death. Evil men would set aside their differences and concentrate on the one Man they hated the most. Christ would be neutralized; He would be taken out of the way so that men could continue in their sins without rebuke or irritation. Peter put it this way, "for truly in this city there were gathered together against your holy servant Jesus, whom you anointed, both Herod and Pontius Pilate, along with the Gentiles and the peoples of Israel, to do whatever your hand and your plan had predestined to take place" (Acts 4:27–28). These are the players on the stage when Christ offered Himself to the people as their Redeemer.

Herod Antipas was the ruler of Galilee; he was the

man who murdered John the Baptist. Herod was probably quite surprised when the guards brought Jesus to him. Even so, the more he questioned Jesus the bolder Herod became, even suggesting that Christ entertain him with a miracle! Christ responded by saying nothing. As has been said, Herod silenced the voice of God! He thought he was judging Jesus but, in fact, it was Jesus who was judging Herod.

Herod mocked Christ and permitted the soldiers to dress Him in an elegant robe. Herod did not issue a final verdict about Jesus, but it was clear that he didn't find Him worthy of death. Still, he was glad to see Him die. Flagrant injustice.

Pontius Pilate was another player on the stage. He was a tragic figure; he knew that Christ was innocent, even wanting to see Him released, but in the end, he handed Him over to the mob. Pilate's wife, bless her, warned him to have nothing to do with Jesus because of a terrifying dream she had the previous night. Pilate, wanting desperately to take his wife's advice, suggested to the people that Christ be set free in accordance with their custom to release a prisoner during the Passover. He would have Jesus flogged then let Him go. But the mob shouted, "Release unto us Barabbas!" (Luke 23:18). As for Christ, they shouted, "Crucify Him! Crucify Him!"

Pilate, faced with the screaming mob, and wanting to

maintain his status with the Jews, granted their request. He washed his hands signifying he wanted nothing to do with the condemnation of this innocent man. Today, he is not remembered for his leadership among the Jews, he's remembered for his cowardice.

Interestingly, Pilate and Herod were enemies, each vying for a privileged position in the Roman pecking order. But Christ united them. "On that very day" we read, "they became friends" (Luke 23:12). Sometimes old animosities have to be set aside to execute a common enemy.

Next, Peter mentions the Gentiles, the Romans who actually carried out the crucifixion. They were, for the most part, indifferent to the squabbles the Jews had with Jesus. The Romans were the occupational troops who were primarily interested in keeping order. But they also wanted to please the Jews whenever they could, upholding the verdict of the Jewish courts. If the authorities wanted Christ to be crucified, so be it. They did the dirty work.

Finally, Peter mentions the "people of Israel." These are the religious leaders who became weary with answering questions about Christ. Though they wanted Christ killed on the grounds of blasphemy, their underlying motive, however, was not theological. Pilate, who had his ear to the ground and who was a keen observer of human nature, knew "that it was out of envy that they had delivered him [Jesus] up" (Matthew 27:18). Put simply, Christ made the religious leaders look bad. Christ had the crowds and the charisma; Christ had the authority and the power.

These are the players on the stage of history who conspired to put Jesus to death. Was there any chance that they would do otherwise? Did God gamble that His Son would actually be killed? Hardly. Peter explains that these people gathered together "to do whatever your hand and your plan had predestined to take place" (Acts 4:28). God saw to it that there was no possibility that His plan would fail. The wicked would do what God marked out beforehand; Christ would die and His death would provide salvation for all who would believe. When man did his worst, God did His best.

Indeed, the very hour that Christ died was predetermined. According to the Hebrew text of the Old Testament, the Passover lamb was slain "between the evenings." Tradition says that this was somewhere in the three hour period between 3:00 p.m. and 6:00 p.m. Notice that these are the hours when Christ became our sin-bearer on that Passover day in Jerusalem, "And about the ninth hour Jesus cried out with a loud voice, saying, "Eli, Eli, lema sabachthani?" that is, "My God, my God, why have you forsaken me?"" (Matthew 27:46). He died on the right day at the right time, just as God had planned.

If we could have interviewed Herod and asked him why he didn't defend Christ, he would not have answered,

"Because I felt the pressure of a divine decree." No, he did as he pleased. Yet in so doing, he was carrying out what God predestined to occur. The same can be said for the other conspirators.

Of course some people object to teaching the sovereignty of God, arguing that it leads to fatalism; and there are probably many examples of this historically. However, if we were to ask Martin Luther, John Calvin, or Jonathan Edwards about the matter, they would say that it is this doctrine that gives us hope in the midst of the doctrinal decay all around us.

A GOSPEL THAT ACTUALLY SAVES

If you wonder what this has to do with the preaching of the gospel in America today, it is simply this: until we understand and preach the doctrine of man's inability to contribute to his salvation, we will always preach a gospel that falls short of the desperate dependence on God that should characterize our witness. We will be satisfied with calling people to Christ without them understanding how desperately they really need Him. Christ will be seen as the remedy for "peace and happiness" rather than the grounds of a sinner's justification before God. Given the kind of gospel preached in our pulpits today, we should not be surprised that the message has lost its power.

Would that Christians in the United States see the great

barrier that God must overcome in saving a sinner! We can do no better than to read the words of the great English preacher, Charles Haddon Spurgeon:

> I shall not attempt to teach a tiger the virtues of vegetarianism; but I shall as hopefully attempt that task as I would try to convince an unregenerate man of the truth revealed by God concerning sin, and righteousness, and judgment to come. These spiritual truths are repugnant to carnal men, and the carnal mind cannot receive the things of God. Gospel truth is diametrically opposed to fallen nature; and if I have not a power much stronger than that which lies in moral suasion [persuasion], or in my own explanations and arguments, I have undertaken a task in which I am sure of defeat...Except the Lord endow us with power from on high, our labour must be in vain, and our hopes must end in disappointment.[2]

Our responsibility is to be true to the message that God, in His gracious mercy, might be pleased to bless. We must exalt the cross since it is there that our salvation was purchased; there God set forth Christ publicly to display His righteousness (see Romans 3:25).

We need to understand that God's compassion will

never cause Him to overlook sin. He must prove that He is just, though He is also "the justifier of those who believe on Jesus" (Romans 3:26). God sent forth Christ to defend His integrity.

The doctrine of justification teaches that God is now free to declare sinners who have believed on Christ as righteous as He Himself is. Indeed, we are credited with the righteousness of Christ. Twenty-four hours a day God demands perfection from His people; twenty-four hours a day, Christ supplies what God demands. When Luther understood this truth, he almost immediately dropped the doctrine of purgatory which taught that few, if any, die righteous enough to enter heaven. Thanks to God, we are *even now* righteous enough to be brought into the very throne room of the Almighty.

At the cross, the love of God was also displayed. After all, God could have kept His justice intact even if Christ had not come to redeem us, but we would have been lost forever. It was not logically necessary that Christ die; the necessity of the cross was based on the compelling power of love.

As we shall see more fully in the next chapter, the wisdom of God was on display at the cross. The dilemma of how sinful human beings could be reconciled to God could not be resolved apart from the divine plan. The cross that was in God's heart became a reality in history.

And we shall yet see the cross in the future.

THE CROSS IN HEAVEN

Some people claim to have peered into heaven, returning to tell us what they have seen. These near-death experiences are most assuredly unreliable and misleading. Certainly, some believers, like Stephen, have looked into heaven before they died, but Satan, in an attempt to deceive, would like to give the same positive experience to unbelievers too. There are, however, some reports which are reliable.

The Apostle John was not near death but very much alive when he had a glimpse into heaven. He writes, "After this I looked, and behold, a door standing open in heaven!" (Revelation 4:1). There he saw God on the throne and heard the worship of the creatures who surrounded Him. But he saw something else too. He saw a scroll, a script that recorded the last years of the history of this world and an angel proclaiming with a loud voice, "Who is worthy to open the scroll and break its seals?" (Revelation 5:2).

John wept because it appeared as if no one was found with the authority to open the scroll. But he could dry his tears, for the Lion of the tribe of Judah was found worthy to read the script and make sure it was followed. Then John writes, "And between the throne and the four living creatures and among the elders I saw a Lamb standing, as though it had been slain, with seven horns and with seven eyes, which are the seven spirits of God sent out into all the earth" (Revelation 5:6).

The cross in heaven!

Just as the body of the resurrected Christ had the nail prints and the scar of the wounded side, so this Lamb appears "as if slain." Far from being an event in the past, the marks of the cross of Christ are found in the center of heaven itself. The cross, someone observed, changed the unchangeable. Heaven itself is different for now that the Lamb has appeared, "they sing a new song."

Notice the lyrics, "Worthy are you to take the scroll and to open its seals, for you were slain, and by your blood you ransomed people for God from every tribe and language and people and nation" (v. 9). If it were not for the cross, these people would not be there. Those who were the objects of God's love for as long as He has existed, can now rejoice. Some have already made their safe arrival in heaven, others are en route. They can rejoice because they have been made a kingdom and priests "and they shall reign on the earth" (v. 10). This is a kingdom that will not be shaken; a kingdom that is unaffected by the chaos that exists on Earth.

"It is not what you know but who you know that matters," we are often told. If this is true on Earth, think of how much more it is true in heaven. For those who know the Lamb, they are the ones who are most blessed. Thus, the heavenly city begins its journey into eternity, separated from the city of man forever.

REVISITING THE CROSS AND THE FLAG

What conclusions can we draw from the primacy of the cross in God's program?

First, *spiritual redemption, not political reformation is at the heart of God's agenda.* The closer we get to the cross, the closer we get to God's heart. Here we see God at His best.

Once we understand the cross, we cannot be satisfied with the civil religion of former President Dwight Eisenhower who said, "Our form of government has no sense unless it is founded in a deeply felt religious faith, *and I don't care what it is*"[3] (italics mine). No, we are not commissioned to call America back to God and religion; we are commanded to call America to God through Christ who died for sinners. Not any religion will do; not any path to God will do.

We should never let the earthly kingdom eclipse the eternal one. Even when we win political and judicial victories—and I pray we will win many—we dare not pin our hopes on such victories no matter how promising the reforms and the possibility of genuine, positive change. Yes, of course, we're not left here to just make the world better, but to make heaven complete! Of course, our task is more difficult than convincing a tiger of the benefits of vegetarianism, but that is why we must trust God to overcome the blindness of the human heart and grant men and women the ability to believe. Nothing should ever divert us from our primary mission.

The early Christians knew their agenda. Though beaten, they continued in boldness. They never questioned the power of the cross to both save and deliver people from their sins. We might become discouraged when we see people who profess faith yet do not follow through. We have all committed enough sins to make us doubt the power of God. But there the cross stands as a reminder of our great need and God's great grace.

Second, *all nations, not just one special nation, compose God's agenda.* There is no special place in heaven for Americans. God desires to have a transnational community. His plan for this cosmos is so much greater than the preservation of the American dream. He desires that there be people redeemed from Russia, Brazil, China, Iraq, Egypt, and so on. God's plan is as great as our world.

Third, *the church, not a political party, is the bearer of God's message.* When Christ said that His light is to be reflected in His followers, "You are the light of the world. A city set on a hill cannot be hidden" (Matthew 5:14), He knew that this light could only come through the gospel not other reforms, no matter how beneficial they may be. Our danger is that we might get used to the darkness rather than let our lights shine even more brightly.

When the moral and spiritual decline of England seemed irreversible, God raised up John Wesley to preach the gospel. During those days, the British Parliament sometimes had to disband at midday because the members were too drunk to continue deliberations. Children worked in factories, rejected and exploited. The revival of the eighteenth century changed that. The transformation of heart brought a transformation of country.

We do not know if God will do the same for America. Clearly, we do not deserve it nor can we insist that He give it to us because "we are His special nation." But perhaps if we confessed our sin of depending on our own clout and turned to Him alone, He might yet be gracious to us, even in this late hour.

When the world was exceedingly wicked, there was Noah.

When the knowledge of the Lord was obliterated from Earth, there was Abraham.

When the people were weary with bondage, there was Moses.

When New England turned away from God, there was Jonathan Edwards.

When we are close to God's heart, we are close to God's power. And when we are close to God's power, we are shining a light in the darkness. Even a candle can cause the darkness in a cave to vanish. The greater the darkness, the more candles are needed. To share the message of the gospel is to rekindle our belief that it is the power of God unto salvation.

A LESSON FROM NAZI GERMANY

Come with me to Stuttgart, Germany, with the nation lying in ruins, and Adolf Hitler about to commit suicide. Helmut Thielicke, a German pastor and theologian, speaks movingly to his congregation, assessing what has gone wrong. In his powerful critique, he explains that the nation had, in effect, gotten what it deserved because it had "repudiated forgiveness and kicked down the Cross of the Lord." Because the cross had been neglected, Germans were blinded, thinking they were special people to God and forgetting that the fist of God had already been raised to "dash them to the ground." He says the church concentrated on political and social problems and overlooked its need for a Redeemer who would set straight the deepest need of their lives.

Then Thielicke came to the heart of the matter, "The denial of God and the casting down of the Cross is never a merely private decision that concerns only my own inner life and my personal salvation, but that this denial immediately brings with it the most brutal consequences for the whole of historical life and especially for our own people. 'God is not mocked.'…The history of the world can tell us terrible tales based on that text."[4] Germany's greatest problem was not political but spiritual; it was not just that their leader was perverse but that the people, for the most part, did not look beyond the earthly kingdom to the heavenly one.

Casting down the cross of Christ!

For that, the church and the country was "crushed by God." Many pastors caved into the political agenda of the day and refused to preach the cross in their ministries. The congregations fell in step, shielding their eyes from the atrocities around them because they refused to humble themselves at the foot of the cross and carry that cross into the world. It is not too strong to say that the failure of many of the German churches can be traced to the loss of the gospel in their life and witness.

Bonhoeffer was right. It is not before us but before the cross that the world trembles.

Footnotes

1. John Stott, *The Cross of Christ* (Downers Grove: Illinois,. InterVarsity Press, 2006), 63.

2. Quoted in Arturo G. Azurdia, *Spirit Empowered Preaching* (Great Britain: Christian Focus Publications, 2015), 14.

3. "And I don't care what it is," Wikipedia, https://en.wikipedia.org/wiki/And_I_don%27t_care_what_it_is

4. Helmut Thielicke and John W. Doberstein, *The Prayer That Spans The World: Sermons On The Lord's Prayer* (Lutterworth Press, 2016).

ERWIN W. LUTZER

CHAPTER FOUR

THE CROSS OF RECONCILIATION

Our culture is fragmenting.

The Founding Fathers believed that the United States was a melting pot; that the diverse ethnic and racial groups would retain their identity but be united with one Constitution as "one nation under God."

John Quincy Adams wrote that immigrants must "cast off their European skin, never to resume it. They must look forward to their posterity, rather than backward to their ancestors."[1] He would, I believe, have been opposed to our present cult of ethnicity which insists that every group should be identified with their past rather than become part of the American "melting pot."

Today we have African Americans, Asian Americans, Hispanic Americans, Anglo Americans, and a host of other groups who want to be identified by their past roots rather than their present status as citizens of the United States. Far from coming together, we seem to be drifting further apart. Add to this our immigration crisis and you realize that we have lost the idea of a cohesive society. In many of our communities, English is the second language.

We are divided economically. We have the rich and the poor, the suburbs and the inner cities. Unfortunately, poverty continues to infest our population and proves resistant to government cures. Despite massive amounts of money for welfare, Medicaid, and subsidized work programs, many are still poor and continue to feel angry and hopeless.

We are divided religiously. We have Protestants, Catholics, Muslims, Hindus, and Buddhists, all of these and others adapting to American culture and competing for the minds and hearts of our population. A Muslim flight attendant complained that her airline is violating her religious beliefs by prohibiting her from wearing a hijab. The U.S. Equal Employment Opportunity Commission agreed and sued the airline for discrimination. With each religious group demanding their "rights," we are indeed a nation in cultural conflict.

We are divided racially. No doubt many university students who sign up for so-called "diversity studies" intend to help bridge racial gaps and bring justice to neglected communities. But unfortunately, these courses too often merely stir up resentment between the oppressed and the oppressors. The argument is that the oppressed and the oppressors must be identified, and only a socialist revolution can make everyone equal. A man who worked with Saul Alinsky, a self-professed radical who wrote *Rules for Radicals*, told me, "Alinsky was not interested in solving problems but rather using them toward his own revolutionary goals." Although Alinsky has been dead for many years, his vision of a cultural Marxist revolution lives on here in the United States.

We are also divided domestically. Family life is disintegrating. The high divorce rate, the escalation of abuse, and the increase in "latchkey" children all testify to the emotional deprivation of this generation. We are living together in a nation that is disconnected, unable to form deep and lasting relationships. In such a world, relationships are either brief high intensity encounters which quickly burn themselves out, or casual relationships that do not fill the human desire for love and a lasting relationship.

Americans are, for the most part, a lonely lot, seeking to fill the void with the latest gadgets or a ski trip. Deep relationships characterized by loyalty and commitment are difficult to maintain by those adults who were not emotionally nourished in the home. Thus, our desires are unmet and, as a nation, we keep turning to those solutions that only inflame greater unmet desires.

To where do we turn?

THE CHURCH, A DOOR OF HOPE

The church is called to model wholesome, caring relationships in a culture that no longer believes that such caring friendships are possible. Our calling is to eschew that part of our culture fueled by a radical individualism that selfishly seeks one's own "good" at the expense of one's neighbor. We have to prove that deep and loyal friendships can exist among those who otherwise have racial, cultural, and economic differences. In other words, we are to model the oneness for which Christ prayed (see John 17:20–23). It is at this very point that we should be most unlike the world.

Sin always divides. When Adam and Eve disobeyed God, they were separated from Him, and later their children were separated from one another. Cain killed Abel and the whole history of the human race was now doomed to fragmentation and broken relationships. When man tried to remain unified by building the tower of Babel, God judged the human race because it strove for unity amid idolatry and personal self-interest.

Let's take an honest look into the human heart.

My pride means that I am better than you and cannot accept you unless you belong to my "tribe." You must conform to my standards of hygiene, diet, and work ethic. If not, I will deem you inferior. No matter how kind I appear to you on the outside, within my heart you are despised. Even if, like the Pharisee, we "thank God that we are not like other men" God even despises the very haughty spirit with which we "thank" Him.

My greed means that you cannot touch what is mine. I have worked for it. And if you do not have the same amount of money I have, you are lazy and mentally challenged. You had better not take what belongs to me, because I will fight for what is mine, no matter how great your need. After all, that is just the American way.

If you appeal to me, if I like your personality and your appearance, if you make me feel good about myself, I will like you. If you begin to drain my emotional energy without making me feel appreciated, I will drop the relationship—the sooner the better. I need relationships that meet my needs, not relationships where I meet the needs of someone else.

Have we not all had such thoughts?

But we might not even be aware of these attitudes that lie coiled like a serpent in the bottom of our hearts. And because America is a large country that offers almost unlimited options, we can live where we like, choose whatever vocation we want, and move from one part of the country to another as it strikes our fancy. This means that we can avoid living and working with those who are different from us. Our prejudices can remain unchallenged.

When my wife and I visited Russia, we learned that often two families would live in the same small apartment due to a severe housing shortage. I can't imagine what it would be like to share the same kitchen, living room, and closets with another family. That certainly would be a challenge to our well-polished personas. In such close quarters where subtle power grabs would be happening every day, the true nature of our hearts would be revealed. I think we'd find ourselves surprised at our own selfishness, anger, and impatience. Friends we dearly love might end up despised living in a close environment with us where petty jealousies and favoritism surface daily.

Thankfully, most of us do not have to live in such conditions in America. But at the same time, it is because of our unlimited options that we have not had to face up to our own prejudices and selfishness. As long as you stay in your corner and I stay in mine, we should be able to get along fine, thank you. And if not, I will move!

God expects more than that. He wants us to be united within our own hearts. Biblical unity is not simply peaceful co-existence. It means I am willing to subject my own personal interests for your good; it means that I can demonstrate love for those whom I, by nature, would despise. It means I am willing to put my life on the line for someone else. It means nothing less than the love of a crucified Savior living in my heart. This is the cross that we are commanded to take into the world.

RETURNING TO THE ONENESS
THAT MADE THE CHURCH GREAT

Think of the hostility that presently exists between Jews and Palestinians. This centuries-old conflict is so deeply rooted in the hearts of those who share the land of Israel that the rules of rationality simply do not apply. A peace treaty might be honored for political necessity, but it will not be honored out of love. No piece of paper can change the human heart. There are no reasons compelling enough to cease the animosity.

Precisely such hatred existed between the Jews and the Gentiles in the first century. The Jews made a fatal error: they thought they were chosen because they were better than others! They forgot that God chose them even though they were "stiff-necked" and otherwise quite unattractive. To be chosen of God should spawn humility, not pride. Religious pride is of the worst kind.

If a Jewish boy married a Gentile girl, or vice versa, a funeral would be held for that Jewish boy or girl. It was forbidden even to help a Gentile mother give birth, since this would be helping another Gentile to be born into the world. To even go to a Gentile house would render the Jew unclean. The Jews withheld the message of reconciliation from the Gentiles and then cursed them for not being chosen! In fact, they said that the Gentles were created to fuel the fires of hell.

The temple existed as a series of courts, each a little higher than the one before. The court of the Gentiles was the farthest from the temple area, with a wall separating them from the inner courts. The sign read, "No foreigner may enter within the barricade which surrounds the sanctuary and enclosure." For a Gentile to enter meant death.

Jews and Gentiles were not just separated religiously, but also racially. When Christ spoke to the woman of Samaria, He broke two taboos simultaneously. Men never spoke to women in Jewish culture, at least they never spoke to an unknown woman with respect. But Christ was also speaking to someone who was racially mixed; she was part Assyrian, which was unforgivable. Jews prided themselves in having Abraham for their father, and to mix Gentile and Jewish blood was more contemptible than being a totally pagan.

Finally, they were separated culturally. The Jews developed their art and symbolism from God's revelation, whereas the Gentiles (such as the Greeks), developed a civilization based on nature and human wisdom. The Jews despised pagan representations and of course, the Gentiles despised the narrow-minded religious fervor of the Jews.

Women in Jewish culture were routinely mistreated, not only barred from the inner sanctuary of the temple area, but also seen as living to serve men. "O God I thank Thee that I am not a woman" Jewish men prayed each day. A woman could be divorced at the whim of her husband, sent away without any due consideration. It was definitely a man's world. A cruel man's world.

The cross changed all this.

LET THE WALLS FALL DOWN

Christ demolished the barriers that existed between competing groups. Paul wrote that Christ broke down "in his flesh the dividing wall of hostility by abolishing the law of commandments expressed in ordinances, that he might create in himself one new man in place of the two, so making peace" (Ephesians 2:14–15).

The wall between Jews and Gentiles best represented by their relationship to the law was destroyed by Christ. The numerous regulations of the Old Testament, with their dietary requirements and priestly functions, stood as a barrier between the two groups. Christ did away with all that, having Himself become the "end of the law for righteousness to everyone who believes" (Romans 10:4). The distinctions which God had made between Jew and Gentile no longer applied.

The warning sign that forbade the Gentiles to enter

into the inner court of the temple had to be set aside once and for all. To dramatize the new era, the veil of the temple was split from top to bottom when Christ died. The cross opened the way for everyone to come to God through the blood that was shed. In the Old Testament, God Himself had told the people to keep their distance from His presence, localized in the Holy of Holies. Now the new message was, "Come! Come on the basis of the cross and come from all corners of the earth!"

Two previously warring groups were made one in Christ. For those who accepted the Messiah, "There is neither Jew nor Greek, there is neither slave nor free, there is no male and female, for you are all one in Christ Jesus. And if you are Christ's, then you are Abraham's offspring, heirs according to promise" (Galatians 3:28–29).

Four times Paul uses that three-letter word "one" in describing the unity between Jew and Gentile. Christ "made us both *one*" (Ephesians 2:14); He created in Himself "*one* new man in place of the two, so making peace" (v. 15); He has reconciled "us both to God in *one* body through the cross, thereby killing the hostility" (v. 16). And "through Him we both have access in *one* Spirit to the Father" (v. 18).

God wounds only that He might heal; He destroys only that He might build. His desire was to create something entirely different, a true core unity between Jew and Gentile. A unity that would be stronger than anything which might divide them. This was a peace treaty that actually changed the hearts of the parties who accepted it. This was a kind of unity that demonstrated the power of God, a unity that was beyond human power and analysis.

Paul gives three figures of speech that help us understand what God did through the cross.

THE CROSS, A NEW CREATION

Amid the clamor of diversity and its emphasis on disunity, amid the finger pointing that blames one race for all the problems in another race, amid the territorialism that exists between neighborhoods, and amid educational differences, God has chosen to create something new. His unity would get to the core of who we are.

First, at the cross He created *a new body* that He "might reconcile us both to God in *one* body" (Ephesians 2:16). In 1 Corinthians 12, Paul uses the imagery of the body, affirming both diversity and interdependence.

How did this unity come about? By the power of the Holy Spirit, through whom we "both have access in one Spirit to the Father" (Ephesians 2:18). God does not have one Holy Spirit for African Americans, another for Asian Americans, and another for Anglo Americans. These are all indwelt by the same Holy Spirit, baptized into the same body. This is a genuine unity because it means we share the same life and are responsive to Christ, the one Head. This body is a unity of accomplishment, where deeds are done together and where sorrows and triumphs are shared.

Second, He created *a new nation.* "So then you are no longer strangers and aliens, but you are fellow citizens with the saints and members of the household of God" (Ephesians 2:19). The church is a new nation no longer dependent on ethnicity or geography.

The entire human race descended from the three sons of Noah: Shem, Ham, and Japheth. Thanks to the cross, descendants from all three were converted. The Apostle Paul, a Shemite, was converted en route to Damascus by a special revelation of Christ. The Ethiopian treasurer, a descendent of Ham was converted though the witness of Philip as he was returning home from Jerusalem. And Cornelius, a descendent of Japheth, was added to the body of Christ when Peter was finally willing to give up his prejudices and enter into the house of a Gentile.

What matters now is not their physical lineage, it is not a matter of blood, for God hath made "from one man [blood] every nation of mankind to live on all the face of the earth, having determined allotted periods and the boundaries of their dwelling place" (Acts 17:26). Hematologists tell us that blood can be transfused across racial lines, it is the one common element. So, ancestry is not what determines our worth as individuals. On this we are all equal.

The unity of believers is now based on the fact that we have been begotten by the same Father in heaven. Christ is our brother and the Holy Spirit is our companion. And this unity takes precedence over all racial histories. We are, says Paul, members of "the household of God."

Thus, the cross speaks to our fragmented society, our disintegrating families. Those who were reared without acceptance and relationships should find their identity in Christ through the church. This is where the weak should be protected, the poor should be helped, and the lonely find friends. This is where there can be genuine unity, borne of love for the same Lord and for one another. In the face of our fragmenting families, we can belong to another family that will seek to meet our needs for acceptance and love.

Christ invites us to His table, as brothers and sisters. When His mother and half-brothers were finding it difficult to get to speak to Him as the crowd was surging around Him, Jesus replied, "'Who are my mother and my brothers?'" And looking about at those who sat around him, he said, 'Here are my mother and my brothers! For whoever does the will of God, he is my brother and sister and mother'" (Mark 3:33–35). The spiritual ties took precedence over blood ties. There is an identity more powerful than that of the human family. It is the family of God.

We know people can unite for various causes: peace, the environment, lower taxes. These coalitions serve their purpose, but when individual interests collide with the cause, the group begins to dissolve. In effect, these are collections of individuals, united for a common goal; it is the agenda that brings them together.

The church is much more than a group of individuals coming together under a common banner. This is more than a union based upon common interests and aspirations. This means even more than the fact that all believers have the same Holy Spirit indwelling them. The Scriptures teach that we actually become one metaphysically, spiritually, internally. The interrelationship is so direct that if one part of the body suffers, the other parts must suffer with it.

Or to say it differently, when we are divided by racism, personality conflicts, and egotistical turf-ism, we not only look bad but the power of God in our lives is diminished. We are tearing at the very fabric of the unity for which Christ prayed. This is a unity where we esteem others better than ourselves. We are grieving the Holy Spirit who disregarded these differences when He saved us.

Spencer Perkins reminds us that there is a difference between integration and reconciliation. Integration is a political concept, reconciliation is spiritual. Integration forced some people to change their behavior. Reconciliation invites the changing of hearts. Would more laws force a change in behavior? Perhaps. But would more laws change behavior in favor of Christ-centered morals and values or against them? What we can know for sure, however, is that our greatest need is a change in the attitude of our heart, and only a spiritual power—God's power—can bring that about.

Perkins talks about the differences he and a white ministry partner had, one so severe that even though they intended to model reconciliation, they were thinking of separating, citing, "irreconcilable differences." But they decided that they would go for counseling one last time to demonstrate that they were "good Christians." He writes, "Neither of us was prepared for the overwhelming simplicity, the complete absurdity, and illogical genius of God's amazing grace." He says that although he knew the meaning of grace from his youth, he never thought of grace as a way of life. He continues, "I knew that we are supposed to love one another as Christ loved us. But somehow it was much easier for me to swallow the lofty untested notion of dying for each other than simply giving grace to brothers and sisters on a daily basis, the way God gives us grace. Maybe I'm dense, but I just never got it." Only by giving one another grace was reconciliation possible. They could either hold to their grievances, insisting that their hurts be redressed, or they could "trust God when we lacked the ability to forgive. We chose grace."[2]

The cross means that we choose grace. Amid the petty judgments of men; amid our many deeply held differences, we must choose to forgive even when not asked. Christ on the cross said, "Father forgive them, for they know not what they do." As Philip Yancey says, "Grace is unfair, which is one of the hardest things about it. It is unreasonable to expect a woman to forgive the terrible things her father did to her, just because he apologizes many years later...Grace, however, is not about fairness."[3]

We are also *a new temple,* built upon the foundation of the apostles and prophets with Christ Jesus Himself being the cornerstone, "in whom the whole structure, being joined together, grows into a holy temple in the Lord. In him you also are being built together into a dwelling place for God by the Spirit" (Ephesians 2:20–22).

During the days of Solomon, workmen went into the quarry and hewed stones that were perfectly shaped for one another. When they were brought to Jerusalem, they were mounted without the sound of a hammer or an axe. God, as it were, goes into the quarry of sin and chooses stones with which He is building His temple. He is the architect, fitting them into the structure as He sees fit. The purpose is not that we might enjoy the music that accompanies our services, nor come to listen to sermons; all of these point to the greater purpose of God, namely, that we might be "built into a dwelling place for God by the Spirit." God is building a place where He might dwell.

When people are introduced to the church, they should

say, "Surely God dwells among these people!" Paul says that the church should have the gift of prophecy so that if an unbeliever enters, "he is convicted by all, he is called to account by all, the secrets of his heart are disclosed, and so, falling on his face, he will worship God and declare that God is really among you" (1 Corinthians 14:24–25).

The cloud of glory that descended into the Holy of Holies during the time of Solomon has long since left. God now resides among His people. When we are gathered in His name to worship, praise, and repent, God is most clearly seen. His agenda is to build a temple of redeemed people where His dwelling can become most evident. This cannot happen unless the stones are unified into a coherent whole, willing to be placed wherever the chief architect desires.

THE HIGH COST OF RECONCILIATION

If the unity of Jew and Gentile cost Christ His life, we cannot expect that our earthly expression of heavenly unity will be easily achieved. It will cost us the hard work of forgiving one another and the humbling of ourselves before the Lord, standing on common ground before Him.

When many Caucasian Christians left the inner cities during the 1960s and 1970s due to property values declining, it was indeed a concession to the city of man against the values of the city of God. Many of our inner cities were left with a great spiritual vacuum as churches God planted in our great population centers moved out to the suburbs. We proved that we were not willing to pay the price of a pilgrim—we'd run when our nest was disturbed.

We, as members of the church, must be willing to break out of our comfort zones and become meaningfully involved in the lives of people who are culturally, racially, and economically different from us. Our commitments must go beyond the superficial. We must be convinced that that which unites us is far stronger than that which can ever divide us.

God reconciles us to Himself and then to each other. If I am reconciled to God and content with His grace, I need no longer be imprisoned in my narrow world. The protective shell which said, "I cannot let you into my heart because it's already filled with myself" now has room for someone else. In fact, there will be room for a lot of other people who don't even have to look like me.

What is the goal to which God is moving? He desires to redeem a transnational community of people who are as diverse as our cosmopolitan cities. If we stand back and look at the bigger picture, we would see dots moving toward the mountain of God. Gazing more closely, we would see that these are human beings, "people from every tribe, and tongue and people and nation" gathering to sing praises to the Lamb. Worthy is the Lamb (see Revelation 5:9).

God's purpose is so much larger than the United States, so much larger than the Western world. God's purpose is to honor Himself by redeeming people from all the diverse tribes of the world. In that company of the redeemed, the racial distinctions will be maintained as proof that God's worldwide purpose was accomplished. But the divisions between the races, the prejudice and mistrust will be gone forever. Gone too will be the feeling of superiority, the belief that some are entitled to a better existence than others because they were born into the right families.

God's redeemed community will reflect the diversity of race; it will show that He honors those who are of "mixed blood." Anyone who calls upon the name of the Lord shall be saved. And our churches today should reflect this agenda.

During World War I, some French soldiers brought the body of a comrade to a cemetery for burial. The priest told them gently that this was a Roman Catholic cemetery, so he needed to ask whether the victim was a Catholic. They answered, no, he was not. The priest was very sorry but if that was the case, he could not permit burial in the church's cemetery. So the soldiers sadly took the body of their friend and buried him just outside the fence of the cemetery.

The next day they returned to mark the grave, but to their astonishment, they couldn't find it. They knew that they had buried him just next to the fence, but the freshly dug soil was not there. As they were about to leave, the priest saw them and said that his conscience troubled him about telling them that they could not bury their friend within the cemetery. So troubled was he that early in the morning he had the fence moved to include the new grave within the parameters of the churchyard.

I tell this story not to minimize the differences between Protestants and Catholics, but rather to show that we as the church must be willing to "move the fences" that so easily separate us. There is little chance that the world will be convinced that God dwells among us unless we are willing to move the fences. Not the doctrinal fences that define our faith (indeed, removing such fences is one of our most serious problems), but those cultural and personal fences that keep the body of Christ divided.

Some of us must move the fence of racism, finally admitting our prejudice and prideful hearts. Some must move the fence of economics, becoming involved in helping the poor rather than being critical of them. Others have to move the barrier of personality or education. We must demonstrate that the unity we have in Christ is much greater than whatever could divide us.

We must all find believers who are different from us and learn to love them for the sake our mutual love for Jesus Christ. We must be willing to put to death the selfishness that keeps us in our own little circles, unwilling to win the good will and trust of our brothers and sisters. Edwin Markim wrote in "Outwitted":

> He drew a circle that shut me out—
> Heretic, rebel, a thing to flout.
> But Love and I had the wit to win;
> We drew a circle that took him in!

As a church we have the responsibility of sharing the good news of Christ with people who are our friends but are not yet our brothers and sisters. They are our neighbors but cannot yet be our prayer partners. We must widen our circles so that through us Christ is represented.

The weak must be protected. The abused healed. The rejected accepted. And the greatest of sinners must, through the church, find forgiveness. The early church was a society of love and mutual care which astonished the pagans and was recognized as something entirely new. It lent persuasiveness to the claim that a new era had dawned in Christ. The Word was not only announced but seen in the community of those who were giving it flesh.

Only through the cross can we show the world what reconciliation looks like. And that unity is such a source of blessing that God uses it to enable the world to believe. "I in them and you in me, that they may become perfectly one, so that the world may know that you sent me and loved them even as you loved me" (John 17:23).

The world can do anything the church can do except

one thing: it cannot show grace. I might add that it cannot show grace because it does not bow before the cross where grace is given to sinners. It can have union, but not unity; self-interest but not selflessness.

Christ has called us to show the way.

Footnotes

1. D.C. McAllister, "What John Quincy Adams Said About Immigration Will Blow Your Mind," *The Federalist,* August 18, 2014, https://thefederalist.com/2014/08/18/what-john-quincy-adams-said-about-immigration-will-blow-your-mind/

2. Spencer Perkins, "Playing the Grace Card," *Christianity Today,* (July 13, 1998), 42–43. https://www.christianitytoday.com/ct/1998/july13/8t8040.html

3. Philip Yancey, *What's So Amazing About Grace?* (Grand Rapids, Michigan: Zondervan, 1997), 80–81.

CHAPTER FIVE

CARRYING THE CROSS INTO A HOSTILE POLITICAL WORLD

When I visited a seminary in St. Petersburg, Russia several years ago, I was asked to give some lectures to students (and some parents) on the subject of prophecy. The discussion turned to the role of the Christian in politics, and as most Americans do, I said that Christians should be involved in the political process. Although I was teaching through an interpreter, I knew immediately that I had wandered into controversial territory. I responded to some questions as best I could then moved on. Only later did my interpreter tell me the reason for the negative reaction: Russian politics is so corrupt that most Christians believe that no Christian can serve in politics with integrity and Christian principles. Virtually every politician they knew or heard about was corrupt and deceitful, usually taking bribes under the table.

The reason that the United States is different is because this country was founded on Christian principles, the separation of powers, and we are still "living on the perfume of an empty Christian vase" as one person put it. Scandals of various kinds are not unknown, of course, and for every scandal we hear about, there are many more hidden beneath the surface.

But today the core values of America are under attack and our country is being transformed. The radical left wants to capture the power structures in America: political, judicial, and cultural, including such things as the media. They believe that capitalism is the source of greed and inequality, and white supremacy is the reason for the continued suppression of minorities. If the state could seize the sources of wealth and power in America, it could put an end to racial inequality and poverty. The state would put curbs on the greedy and the gap between the haves and the have-nots could be bridged. Everyone would be living quite contentedly in the utopian vision of cultural Marxism.

We know better.

Revolutionizing America according to socialist principles would not put an end to greed and self-seeking. Corruption, far from disappearing, would be more widespread and the heavy hand of government would intrude upon our freedoms. Equality in a socialist society would, of necessity, mean the end of the free speech and freedom of religion. Both history and human nature testify to the oppression of a socialist state. Eventually, we would agree with the believers in Russia: politics is too corrupt for Christians to pursue as a career.

But the day is coming when we can expect such a doomsday scenario. Socialism is attractive, especially for young adults. Imagine free tuition, free health care, and "income equality" no matter the job you have. So, inch by inch, law by law, and election by election, we are headed toward more government control in our economy, in our schools, in our healthcare, and the looming "climate change" proposals.

Hitler, a master of propaganda, said that in the political world, opponents must be demonized; nothing good thing can ever be said about them. "Hate" he said, "was better than mere dislike." Polarization is the key to revolution. Today, outrage fuels our debates while civility and reason are but memories.

Living for Christ in the United States is not going to be the easy ride it has been. Tough decisions will have to be made; churches will be told they'd better get with the LGBTQ agenda or face endless and expensive legal challenges. Parents who homeschool their children might be deemed too "intolerant" to be trusted with their offspring. Christians at our universities will not be *talked* out of their faith but *mocked* out of their faith—shamed into silence.

It is into this world that we must carry the cross—and

not just any cross, but the cross of Christ. Someone has well said that it is easy for us to pick up our cross and carry it until we realize where it's leading us. In his book, *The Cost of Discipleship,* Dietrich Bonhoeffer said, "When Christ calls a man, he bids him come and die." The cross leads us to Golgotha.

The purpose of this chapter is to better understand what the suffering of the cross meant to Jesus so that we might better understand what it should mean for us. His challenge to us is not just to attend church, putting a few dollars in the offering basket then return home to resume business as usual. The challenge to carry His cross is a lifestyle, one that may include possible ridicule and painful sacrifice.

We may not yet be living in Russia or the intolerant and violent Middle East, but there is already faint handwriting on the wall. No nation on Earth has sinned against as much light as America.

Our days of freedom may be numbered.

LOOKING LIKE OUR REDEEMER

Friedrich Nietzsche, the philosopher who paved the way for Hitler by proclaiming "the death of God" and predicting the coming of a superman who would return Germany to greatness by force, wrote scathing denunciations of Christianity. In *Thus Spoke Zarathustra,* the protagonist rages against Christians saying, "to make me believe in their Redeemer: more redeemed would his disciples have to appear!"

Perhaps Nietzsche had no right to ask Christians to "look like their Redeemer" since he so vehemently hated the very values "their Redeemer" espoused in His "Sermon on the Mount." Nietzsche believed that love and meekness is exactly what Germany did *not* need. It would not be the meek who would inherit the earth, but the vengeful and powerful.

Inconsistencies aside, Nietzsche's quote is a forceful reminder that if we want people to believe in our Redeemer, we most assuredly should look and act redeemed. This leads us to ask: What should make Christians stand out in this world? At what points should we be most unlike the world? What does it mean to carry our cross in an age in which the cross has been emptied of its meaning?

The cross represents a great "value-reversal." The cross stands as a permanent witness to the fact that what men hate, God loves, and what God loves, men hate. The cross should make us recognizable in the world. Bearing our cross should be the one indisputable mark of a redeemed life. The world *is* watching.

When the world sees us, they should be surprised, taken aback, and forced to take note. We should live as though from another realm with a different set of values, different aspirations, and a different interpretation of life itself. Just as Christ was both loved and hated; obeyed and reviled, so we should be in the world. "Remember the word that I said to you: 'A servant is not greater than his master.' If they persecuted me, they will also persecute you. If they kept my word, they will also keep yours" (John 15:20).

We have benefited from a Christian-friendly government, but those days may well be behind us. We are entering a path not tread by Americans before.

At no point is Christ so clearly our example as when the nails pierced His hands and feet. "For to this you have been called, because Christ also suffered for you, leaving you an example, so that you might follow in his steps. He committed no sin, neither was deceit found in his mouth. When he was reviled, he did not revile in return; when he suffered, he did not threaten, but continued entrusting himself to him who judges justly" (1 Peter 2:21–23).

Sadly, the world often does not see the cross, and cynical skeptics watch us like hawks especially when our walk and our talk do not match. Sometimes the church hides the very cross it is asked to carry into the world; worse, the cross is actually besmirched, and the world feels justified in its rebellion.

Too often we look very *un*redeemed.

CHRISTIANS, POLITICS, AND THE CROSS

WHEN THE WORLD CANNOT SEE
THE CROSS

Too often we are not a steppingstone but a stumbling block to the world.

I don't need to go to great lengths to make the point that the church is sometimes its own worst enemy. We have often squandered our influence by being led by abusive pastors, selfish turf-ism, and moral failure. In a world of social media, every flaw is exposed and read around the world. What used to be a local failure known only within a given community is now given national attention.

If you judge a church only by its critics, none can stand. Some churches are like a circular firing squad where members shoot at each other, each using verses of Scripture to justify their positions—and looking nasty to the world.

We can only respond to such skirmishes by seeking God for discernment. Some "church fights" are necessary, some are not. We need to know the difference between a cause that merits exposure and even division and those that must be handled privately and locally.

My point is that if we act like the world by asserting our "rights" and by being defensive and finger-pointing, we jeopardize our witness. To put it more clearly, if we don't humbly deal with obvious kinds of abuses in the church, we give the world no reason to believe on our Christ.

To paraphrase Nietzsche again, "If we want people to

believe on our Redeemer, we should look redeemed." That kind of witness cannot happen without deep prayer and repentance—and a reevaluation of our priorities.

What are those qualities that should be attractive to a skeptical world?

CHRIST: OUR EXAMPLE IN A HOSTILE WORLD

The Jewish world of Christ's time was filled with hostility: hostility toward the Romans, hostility toward the Gentiles, and eventually hostility toward Christ Himself. Jesus was born into a world that did not receive Him, a world that ended up crucifying Him.

What characteristics did Christ display in the midst of controversies, misunderstandings, open defiance, and unjust suffering? He modeled godliness in the midst of an ungodly world. He calls us to do the same.

THE HUMILITY OF CHRIST

Christ's change of location from heaven to Earth represents the greatest act of condescension. He embarked on a slope that would take Him from the heights to the depths. And if we represent Him well, we will follow in His footsteps. If we want to look redeemed, we should have the humility of our Redeemer.

Let's ponder this well-known passage:

"Have this mind among yourselves, which is yours in Christ Jesus, who, though he was in the form of God, did not count equality with God a thing to be grasped, but emptied himself, by taking the form of a servant, being born in the likeness of men" (Philippians 2:5–7). Jesus existed in the form (Greek, *morphe*) of God; now He exists in the form (*morphe*) of a servant.

In heaven, Christ gave orders; on Earth, He would receive them. He who received the adulation of the heavenly hosts, would now be mocked, falsely accused, and sometimes ignored. He who owned all things, would now not have a suit of clothes or a home He could call His own.

What might He have looked like if we could have seen Him before Bethlehem? We need only read the words of Isaiah who did see Him. "In the year that King Uzziah died I saw the Lord sitting upon a throne, high and lifted up; and the train of his robe filled the temple" (Isaiah 6:1). Angels surrounded the throne, calling to each other, "Holy holy, holy, is LORD of hosts; the whole earth is full of his glory" (v. 3). Jesus actually was God, He wasn't just applying for the job.

This equality with God was not something at which Christ "grasped;" that is, He did not hold on to His position, insisting on His right to enjoy heaven without interruption. He emptied Himself and became a servant. He didn't volunteer to be God; but He did volunteer to be a servant. He became humble even though He had nothing to be humble about.

In order to be a servant, Christ had to live as a man dependent on God the Father. He said that He did nothing by His own initiative and strength but did only what the Father wanted Him to do. It was all voluntary, of course, for He still possessed the attributes of deity.

Christ did not have to accept such humiliation and the abuse that went along with it. He didn't leave the courts of heaven because He was fired, He was not squeezed out because of a restructuring move within the Godhead. *He chose the downward slope.*

Now He was shouted at, "Get out of the way!" or "We know who you are, a carpenter's son!" He sometimes walked fifty miles in one week, often with scant supplies and virtually no protection from the weather. This was not the role to which He was accustomed.

We can't understand this. We tend to clutch position and power until our knuckles turn white. We fight when we are demoted; we stand on our rights and threaten legal action. We gossip and criticize; we try to manipulate people and circumstances in order to "even the score." We become angry and resentful, unwilling to see ourselves as others do. But if we want to look redeemed, we should above all people, be genuinely humble. We don't hire an attorney when we are fired (especially in a church), even if unjustly.

We should be more eager to use the courts to defend the rights of others than we are to defend our own.

When others fall into sin, we "restore him in a spirit of gentleness. Keep watch on yourself, lest you too be tempted" (Galatians 6:1). Of course, we should not cover up abuse or give superficial suggestions to wrongdoers. But if we want to be like Christ, we must confess a dictatorial, self-protective, and judgmental spirit for the sin it is. I've even known pastors who are arrogant, envious, and have a spirit of entitlement. They have not made Jesus attractive to their flock and to the watching world.

The world doesn't have many opportunities to see us as servants. We must do all we can to meet the needs of suffering people. We must, like Christ, be seen walking among the people of the world doing good. Whenever possible, we should go to great lengths to not polarize the very people who need to hear the message we have to share.

Someone has said that many men have aspired to become gods. Indeed, the Romans took an emperor and declared him to be god. But only once in history did a God aspire to become a man.

We have something to be humble about! We are sinners. We must come to the place where we realize that whatever good there is in us is implanted by God. If we are as selfish as the world, if we angrily insist on our rights and make a spectacle of the insults we receive, either real or imagined, we will be indistinguishable from our culture. The world is not impressed when we malign them with overtones of political self-interest or distort their political views. We must remember that at the end of the day, what the world needs most is to see Jesus.

Humility is not an enemy of truth.

I certainly don't want to imply that we roll over and play dead when we are discredited, lied about, or if our rights are violated. We do not become doormats. We might protest and argue our case, but we do so with fairness, a loving spirit, and a caring heart. We are able to endure injustice with dignity because we see it as a badge of honor. "For this is a gracious thing, when, mindful of God, one endures sorrows while suffering unjustly. For what credit is it if, when you sin and are beaten for it, you endure? But if when you do good and suffer for it you endure, this is a gracious thing in the sight of God" (1 Peter 2:19–20). Not once did Jesus back away from speaking the truth when truth was needed. Nor should we.

I believe Christians should be in all levels of society and in various available vocations. Wherever they are positioned, there they must stand for Christ. And when told they must compromise their convictions, they must draw a line in the sand and say, "I can do this, but I can't do *that*." Then, like Christians throughout the centuries, they must be willing to face the consequences.

Let's approach our political, cultural, and racial differences with "humble strength." We don't claim to have all the answers; we only claim that we know the One who does have the answer to our deepest needs, and we live and speak on His behalf.

Let us never compromise our convictions, but let our actions mirror the humility of Jesus. When standing up for Jesus, let us never lose sight of the fact that we must look like our redeemer.

THE SUFFERING OF CHRIST

Christ went from Victor to Victim.

He was "obedient to the point of death, even death on a cross" (Philippians 2:8). There were many ways to die; crucifixion was reserved for the bad guys, it was the chosen method for the criminals, the rabble-rousers. It was a curse to hang on a cross. Christ was so cursed.

He went from the crown to the cross. From being in charge to allowing others to take charge. Jesus permitted the devil to do his work. Jesus looked His enemies in the eye and said, "But this is your hour, and the power of darkness" (Luke 22:53). And yet with such humility, He changed the world.

Political power did not do it. Not by ushering in a kingdom in which the subjects would have to obey—that kingdom is yet future. Instead, Jesus chose to concentrate on the hidden kingdom, the transformation of lives. And so should we.

Salvation was brought about by suffering, not ruling.

Christ did not change the world through His miracles, but by His suffering. His miracles, His "signs," helped only a few people, and even those restored to health had to eventually die. "Christ," someone has said, "did miracles and did not advertise them; today, people advertise miracles and do not do them." His suffering did what miracles could not. Likewise, our suffering can represent Christ to a selfish world.

Back in February of 2015, ISIS militants overran thirty villages that make up the Khabur River Valley in Syria. They bombed and destroyed twelve churches. They kidnapped 250 Assyrian Christians. Seven months later, they dressed three of these captured residents in orange jumpsuits and videotaped their execution. In captivity, with guns to their heads the Christians did not convert to Islam despite the fact that families scattered, children died, and women were raped.[1] For them, carrying their cross was not a doctrine to be lauded, it was a reality to be practiced.

We may never understand why this happened, but as Christians we can trust that these believers did not suffer and die in vain. They believed that "the sufferings of this present time are not worth comparing with the glory that is to be revealed to us" (Romans 8:18). And thankfully, their evil murderers will be brought to justice (see Revelation 6:9–11).

As Americans, most of us are loath to suffer for our faith; we think that we should be able live for Christ and be accepted, perhaps even applauded. But the freedoms we take for granted are being challenged in our courts and in our media-driven culture. The day is coming when we will no longer simply proclaim the gospel with our mouths but will be asked to authenticate it by our willingness to suffer.

Michael Baumgarten, a nineteenth century Lutheran pastor who was excommunicated because of his adherence to the true gospel wrote, "There are times in which lectures and publications no longer suffice to communicate the necessary truth. At such times the deeds and sufferings of the saints must create a new alphabet in order to reveal again the secret of truth."[2] Suffering communicates the gospel in a new language; it authenticates the syllables that flow so easily from our lips. When the chaff is separated from the wheat, the kernels germinate and grow.

Are we willing to be fired from our jobs because of our deeply held convictions? Are we willing to be shamed for what we believe? Ostracized? Willing to endure lies and false accusations? Jesus taught us that holiness leads to suffering. For Him, that suffering ended on a cross.

THE COMPASSION OF CHRIST

Christ cared.

Jesus suffered, yes, but He also cared. More precisely, *He suffered because He cared.* He bore the burdens of others in a way that was tender and compelling. Whether He was holding children in His arms or speaking words of forgiveness to a prostitute, Jesus, even today, is "touched with the feelings of our infirmities."

We should care enough to take upon ourselves the burdens of others that we could easily avoid. This reflects the suffering of those who identified with the Jews in Nazi Germany when they could have remained silent; the suffering chosen by the person who adopts a special needs child; the suffering of the one who sacrifices his career for the challenge of missionary work in a remote jungle. Chosen suffering, I believe, is most precious to God. This is the suffering Christ endured on our behalf.

Have we ever chosen to suffer on behalf of others? Jesus expects us to. Even though I believe that Christ's words apply to a future time, they speak to us today. Read these chilling words of rebuke:

"Then he will say to those on his left, 'Depart from me, you cursed, into the eternal fire prepared for the devil and his angels. For I was hungry and you gave me no food, I was thirsty and you gave me no drink, I was a stranger and you did not welcome me, naked and you did not clothe me, sick and in prison and you did not visit me.' Then they also will answer, saying, 'Lord, when did we see you hungry or thirsty or a stranger or naked or sick or in prison, and did not minister to you?' Then he will answer them, saying, 'Truly, I say to you, as you did not do it to one of the least of these, you did not do it to me'" (Matthew 25:41–45).

Do we want to show hospitality to Christ? Do we want to visit Him in prison and get Him medical help when needed? Expending ourselves for others will do more for the cause of Christ than anger and shouting louder than those who oppose us.

Bonheoffer asked his generation, "Who is Jesus Christ for us?" For him it was the Jews. They were Christ to him.

So, who is Christ for us?

- The unborn child and the terrified teenager who knows not where to turn.
- The single mother who needs someone to give her son a male role model.
- The biracial child who is ridiculed because of his/her features.
- The young man who struggles with same-sex attraction or even fears he might be "trans."
- The inmates in a local prison who have no one to visit them.
- The poor in our inner cities.

These are just a few who are Christ to us today. But so is our alderman, the president, the mayor, and the cab driver. Everyone who crosses our path is Christ to us. At a religious festival in Brazil there was a sign "Cheap Crosses for Sale." Just so, we often want a cross that is easy to carry, a cross that doesn't require us to scale down our lifestyle. We are looking for a bargain. But only the cross of Christ will do if we are to accept Nietzsche's challenge to look like our Redeemer.

There's a story about a pilgrim making his way to the Promised Land. He was carrying his master's cross, a burden he cheerfully accepted. He noticed that the further he walked, the heavier it became. As the pilgrim became weary, he sat down to rest and noticed a woodsman nearby. "Good friend" the pilgrim called, "Could I use your axe to shorten my cross?" The woodsman complied.

The pilgrim traveled on, making much progress. The cross was shorter, his burden lighter. Soon the Promised Land was in sight. Drawing near, however, he noticed that a deep gulf separated him from the glories beyond. He would use the cross to span the divide.

Though he struggled mightily to span the divide with the cross, it fell short by the very amount he had removed. Just then the pilgrim awoke; it was just a dream. And now with tears streaming down his face, he clutched his cross to his breast, and pressed on. The cross was just as heavy, but its burden was lighter.

I need not point out that we do not enter heaven by "carrying our heavy cross" but by trusting in Christ for our salvation. That said, we are to carry our cross if we are to have an abundant entrance into the Promised Land.

At this point in the United States, Christians can still enter the political world without compromising their convictions. But as we slide into humanistic values where power, not principle, is the driving agenda, we will have to take our place with our brothers and sisters in other countries who are called to carry their cross at great personal sacrifice.

There are two things we can do as we see the rising persecution. We can angrily denounce our enemies or we can prudently choose to carry the full weight of Christ's cross. *The lighter our cross, the weaker our witness.*

Bishop Samuel, who died in a hail of gunfire with Anwar Sadat of Egypt back in the early 1980s, told Dr. Ray Bakke how Christianity captured northern Africa in the early centuries. He spoke about the love of the Christians that defied explanation. For example, in those days, there were no abortion procedures, so unwanted children were just left to die on the streets. And since there were no baby bottles, nursing mothers gathered in the town square while young men went on "baby runs" seeking abandoned infants. The babies were brought to the nursing mothers who adopted them as their own.

Also, since Christians were often discriminated against, they were given lowly positions such as garbage collectors. When they came across dead bodies (often as the result of a plague) the Christians would wash the bodies and give them a decent burial, arguing that even the wicked deserve a burial in light of the coming resurrection. It was such acts of love that captured the minds of the pagans; they were impressed by a supernatural love, a love of service even to the people of the world. And with their hearts, they won North Africa to the Christian faith.

Yes, Nietzsche, for all of his insanities, had one thing right: if Christians expect people to believe in their Redeemer, they are going to have to look more redeemed. And standing at the center of this redemption is accepting the cross as a way of life.

Since we have a Redeemer whose love compelled Him to die a horrible death for us, we should not expect our cross to be light. Let us take up our cross in humble repentance and "look redeemed." Only when we do that will we be "worthy" of Him.

"Whoever loves father or mother more than me is not *worthy* of me, and whoever loves son or daughter more than me is not *worthy* of me. And whoever does not take his cross and follow me is not *worthy* of me. Whoever finds his life will lose it, and whoever loses his life for my sake will find it" (Matthew 10:37–39, italics added).

Only a heavy cross is "worthy" of Christ followers.

Footnotes

1. A fuller account of these horrid events is found in "Survivors in a Great War" by Mindy Belz in the March 16, 2019 edition of *World Magazine.* https://world.wng.org/2019/02/survivors_in_a_great_war

2. Cited in Eberhard Bethge, *Bonhoeffer: Exile and Martyr* (New York: Seabury, 1975), 155.

ERWIN W. LUTZER

CHAPTER SIX

THE TRIUMPH OF THE CRUCIFIED

"What will happen if the radical political left gains even more power in Washington?" a Christian activist asked me. The answer, of course is: *"perhaps the kingdom of God will do very well, thank you."*

Not until we understand the difference between the kingdom of God and the kingdom of man will we escape the pessimism that so often characterizes those who see the demise of God's kingdom in every downward turn of human events. Yes, the kingdom of God did quite well under the likes of Nero and even under Mao Zedong after the communist victory in China in 1949. When Christ said that He would build His church and the gates of Hades "could not prevail against it," we can be sure that it would take much more than electing the wrong president to thwart God's purposes.

Let me be clear: persecution is not always a blessing. Sometimes it has destroyed churches and marginalized their witness. But that being said, we must remember that the church does not need political structures to keep it propped up; certainly God uses the economic, social, and political powers of the day to further His purposes, but at times the church has to survive on its own, surrounded by a hostile culture and government. We are heartened by the words of C.S. Lewis, "Nations, cultures, arts, civilizations—these are mortal, and their life is to ours as the life of a gnat."[1]

We have stressed that our responsibility is to share the Good News of the cross before the watching world. But why should we be optimistic about the eventual outcome? The answer is that Christ is indeed Lord of the kingdoms, even today. And there is no event that so portrays the triumph of Christ than His Ascension into heaven and His predicted return.

Given the curtain that divides us from the hereafter, it's not surprising that the writings of virtually all of the leading religions are silent about the present responsibilities of their dead leaders. The most devout Muslim will admit that he really doesn't know what Muhammad has been doing during these many centuries, though he is believed to be in paradise. Hindus can only guess what role Krishna plays on the other side of the grave. The same goes for the followers of Bahaullah, Zoroaster, and other religions. Not only is the present existence of these leaders unclear, but so are their plans for the future.

Christians, however, know exactly what Jesus is doing today and what He is planning for the future. We get to read the last chapter that describes a scene that is both chilling and yet triumphant.

As we shall see, the greatest geopolitical system ever devised on Earth is still to come. The worldwide rule and worship of a political ruler will someday dwarf any kings or rulers of the past. We could say, "Move over Stalin, Hitler, and Mao Zedong. Make way for a political statesman more evil than all of you combined!" Enter the antichrist. He is still to arise out of this world and will win his kingdom in defiance of Christ. He will slaughter all opposition, bask in worldwide acclaim, and finally bring a measure of stability to a conflicted world. Totalitarianism on steroids.

But not for long.

The rightful King of the universe who ascended to heaven from the Mount of Olives will return as promised. This will spell the end of politics as we know it.

THE ASCENSION OF CHRIST

Before we speak about the return of Christ and His victory over all political and religious enemies, we must remind ourselves of the triumph of His Ascension. Given Christ's credentials, we should not be surprised that we not only have details about His bodily ascension into heaven, but a description of what He is doing today and what His plans are for tomorrow. Ultimately, He is King, not just over the city of God, but also the city of man. He has no serious rivals in the universe. But I'm ahead of the story.

Let's read Luke's account: "And when he had said these things, as they were looking on, he was lifted up, and a cloud took him out of their sight. And while they were gazing into heaven as he went, behold, two men stood by them in white robes, and said, 'Men of Galilee, why do you stand looking into heaven? This Jesus, who was taken up from you into heaven, will come in the same way as you saw him go into heaven'" (Acts 1:9–11).

Christ went up, that is, His body actually left Earth and moved toward the sky. He entered the atmospheric heavens and disappeared in a cloud. He took a journey that involved space and time; His body didn't vanish, it moved upward from the Mount of Olives until it disappeared beyond human sight. He actually "passed through the heavens" (Hebrews 4:14).

Heaven is both a place and a state. As a state, heaven represents an entirely different order of reality. Its occupants can apparently traverse great distances in an instant, unhindered by the spatial limitations that curtail our travel plans. At the Ascension, Jesus went from one mode of existence to another—from the material world to the spiritual world, from the finite world to the infinite world. We don't know the coordinates of heaven, but we can say, thanks to eyewitnesses, that He left Earth gradually, visibly, and bodily.

En route to heaven, Christ might well have been beset with the concentrated opposition of Satan and all of his hosts. Passing through the atmosphere, "the prince of the power of the air" would have launched another of his many desperate but fruitless attacks against the Son of God. Christ sustained these without any hint of failing. His victory had already been accomplished.

When the God-man stepped back into the glories of heaven, no one questioned His right to enter. He didn't come pleading for mercy. No mediator had to open the door for Him. He was not receiving a privilege that was beyond His rights. He was simply returning home after a painful but successful journey.

Today Christ, in perfect manhood, is in the midst of the throne room in heaven. His glory is like that on the Mount of Transfiguration: He is ablaze with blinding light. His humanity joined to deity gave Him special rights. He always had these rights as the Son of God, now He has them as the Son of Man as well. Paul described Christ as ascending "far above all rule and authority and power and dominion, and above every name that is named, not only in this age but also in the one to come" (Ephesians 1:21). He arrived as the undisputed ruler of the universe.

Think of this: Christ will never increase in strength,

for He is already *omnipotent;* He will never increase His knowledge, for He is already *omniscient;* He will never be given a larger kingdom, for He is already *omnipresent.* He's not waiting to be crowned king, but He is waiting to be recognized as King. Having completed redemption, "he sat down at the right hand of God, waiting from that time until his enemies should be made a footstool for his feet" (Hebrews 10:12–13).

Yes, He rules even while He waits.

Why does He wait? He's letting history prove a point—namely, that man cannot rule the world. He is also waiting for the company of the redeemed to be completed. He has delegated His rule to the kings and princes of this world, letting them exercise their authority as they see fit. Their influence, however, is limited by the divine will and purpose so that we can confidently say that God's will is being done on Earth. History is marching toward a goal.

Be clear about this: Christ is just as much King when He is waiting as when He is winning! He is just as much King in His ascent as He will be at His descent. He is just as much in control in heaven as He will be on Earth. For now, He is content to direct the affairs of Earth through erring representatives; He is willing to let Satan roam Earth like a criminal who has skipped bail.

For now, the rebels have taken over the premises. But the day will come when the only King whom God recognizes will be acknowledged by every tongue ever created. "Therefore God has highly exalted him and bestowed on him the name that is above every name, so that at the name of Jesus every knee should bow, in heaven and on earth and under the earth, and every tongue confess that Jesus Christ is Lord, to the glory of God the Father" (Philippians 2:9–11).

Let the politicians of this world exercise their authority and wield their power. Let the armies of Earth persecute God's children. Let the world's religious leaders rise up and assert that their claims are as valid as those of Jesus Christ. Let the evolutionists deny the existence of a Creator and raise their fists against natural law in spite of the fact that "his invisible attributes, namely, his eternal power and divine nature, have been clearly perceived, ever since the creation of the world" (Romans 1:20).

All will be raised to give account before God's Supreme Court.

THE GLORIOUS RETURN OF CHRIST

When Christ returns in glory to the Mount of Olives, He will find a world unified in opposition to His rule. The beast and false prophet will be in full control. What they don't know is that their authority was exercised only by the permission of God. And what awaits them will end politics as we know it.

God has an answer for worldwide rebellion: Christ's rule over the world.

Let those who espouse sexual freedom flaunt their influence, the time will come when they will give an account and be judged by a different standard. "Though they know God's righteous decree that those who practice such things deserve to die, they not only do them but give approval to those who practice them" (Romans 1:32). Let them shout their slogans and demand their "rights" because when the King comes their deception will be exposed.

Here is a question: "Why do the nations rage and the peoples plot in vain? The kings of the earth set themselves, and the rulers take counsel together, against the LORD and against his Anointed, saying, 'Let us burst their bonds apart and cast away their cords from us.'"

Here is the answer: "He who sits in the heavens laughs; the Lord holds them in derision….'As for me, I have set my King on Zion, my holy hill.'" (Psalm 2:1–4; 6). God's answer to man's rebellion is the enthronement of Christ.

The passing kingdoms of Earth will give way to the eternal Kingdom of God. Jesus will reign not by winning a democratic election, but because of who He is and what He accomplished. He will rule by divine right. "The kingdom of the world has become the kingdom of our Lord and of his Christ, and he shall reign forever and ever" (Revelation 11:15).

Presently, the world has room for many kings but in the end, all will acknowledge the authority of King Jesus. In the New Jerusalem, "the kings of the earth will bring their glory into it" (Revelation 21:24). All the glory of others will be laid at the feet of King Jesus.

Jesus has the authority to exercise judgment, and He will act.

A word that is on the minds of many today is *justice.* There is "marriage justice" (same-sex marriage); there is "reproductive justice" (abortion), "racial justice," and "economic justice." These various versions of justice are often all grouped, without regard to any distinction between them, under the general heading of "social justice."

No doubt we will discover that Jesus Christ's view of justice is very different than ours; we have some hints in the Bible, but only the Sovereign Lord will balance the scales perfectly.

Around the world, women are being raped and children are being abused. In some parts of the world, famine is killing thousands of people every day. In our own country, marriages are being torn apart, drugs are destroying children. Who can comprehend the terror, the fear, and the buckets of tears shed every hour on this hapless planet? Why would the King allow His kingdom to be overtaken by rebels?

We have this assurance: "We give thanks to you, Lord

God Almighty, who is and who was, for you have taken your great power and begun to reign. The nations raged, but your wrath came, and the time for the dead to be judged, and for rewarding your servants, the prophets and saints, and those who fear your name, both small and great, and for destroying the destroyers of the earth" (Revelation 11:17–18).

"And I saw the dead, great and small, standing before the throne, and books were opened. Then another book was opened, which is the book of life. And the dead were judged by what was written in the books, according to what they had done" (Revelation 20:12).

Everyone will be judged by what they did with what they knew and the opportunities they had. Those who never heard about the sacrifice of Christ will be judged in accordance with the light of nature and their own conscience. The judgment will be fair and righteous.

Throughout all of eternity we will affirm, "Just and true are your ways, O King of the nations!" (Revelation 15:3).

The perpetrators of martyrdom will be judged.

By some estimates, about 400 Christians a day are being martyred for their faith, particularly those who live in the Middle East. Such martyrs are waiting for justice. And they will have it. "When he opened the fifth seal, I saw under the altar the souls of those who had been slain for the word of God and for the witness they had borne. They cried out with a loud voice, 'O Sovereign Lord, holy and true, how long before you will judge and avenge our blood on those who dwell on the earth?'" (Revelation 6:9–10).

The killers will get their due, both on Earth and in eternity. Every deception exposed, every false religion called into account, and every cruelty addressed. The martyrs in Revelation were told to rest a little longer until others joined their ranks. But the perpetrators will be brought to justice.

Be patient. The scales will be balanced.

Antichrist will be judged.

The day is coming when there will be a political/religious ruler who will be a direct threat to Jesus Christ's earthly rule. He will capture the nations and mesmerize the leaders of the world and force them to bow to his undisputed sovereign rule. The antichrist, called "the beast," will be given worldwide authority and supernatural powers. "And authority was given it over every tribe and people and language and nation, and all who dwell on earth will worship it, everyone whose name has not been written before the foundation of the world in the book of life of the Lamb who was slain" ("Revelation 13:7–8).

Visualize an evil demonically controlled "beast" receiving worldwide worship and promoted by a false prophet. He uses economics to deprive people of food and shelter unless they have his mark—a sign of their allegiance to him. Those who refuse the mark, will be killed with the sword.

Chilling.

But justice is coming. "And the beast was captured, and with it the false prophet who in its presence had done the signs by which he deceived those who had received the mark of the beast and those who worshiped its image. These two were thrown alive into the lake of fire that burns with sulfur. And the rest were slain by the sword that came from the mouth of him who was sitting on the horse [Jesus], and all the birds were gorged with their flesh" (Revelation 19: 20–21).

The evil rulers are left with nothing but an eternity of suffering and regret. Justice arrived: swift, accurate, and much deserved.

OUR PARTICIPATION IN CHRIST'S VICTORY

This book has shown the conflict between politics and the cross, between earthly kingdoms and the heavenly kingdom. We have discussed our duty of fulfilling our responsibility to both spheres. We know that there are no easy answers in this fallen world.

Sometimes we win in politics and sometimes we lose. Either way, believers are assured of arriving in the heavenly kingdom and God will raise "us up with him and seat us with him in the heavenly places in Christ Jesus" (Ephesians

2:6). You and I as believers are already in heaven, heirs to an incredible inheritance.

Christ promised that He would prepare a place for us. There is a crown that only you can wear, a mansion that only you can enter. Peter said there is a place "reserved in heaven for you" (1 Peter 1:4, KJV). The only way I can be cast out of heaven is if Christ Himself is thrown out! He is representing me, protecting my interests, even at this very moment.

What Christ has by divine right was purchased for us by divine mercy. We will never become what He is, but we shall enjoy what He has. We stand amazed at the wonder of God's grace. "And night will be no more. They will need no light of lamp or sun, for the Lord God will be their light, and they will reign forever and ever" (Revelation 22:5).

About ten times in the New Testament, Christ is said to be "seated at the right hand of God the Father." The imagery is important. In the Old Testament, priests who offered sacrifices were not allowed to sit. They worked in eight-hour shifts, standing the whole time; to sit down would mean that their work was finished.

Christ, though seated at the right hand of God the Father, does occasionally stand.

When angry men were preparing to stone Stephen, even before the stones began to fly, we read, "But he, full of the Holy Spirit, gazed into heaven and saw the glory of

God, and Jesus standing at the right hand of God. And he said, 'Behold, I see the heavens opened, and the Son of Man standing at the right hand of God'" (Acts 7:55–56).

Christ was not too busy to notice one of His servants about to experience the pain of martyrdom. Whatever else may have been happening on the planet at that moment, Stephen had Christ's full attention. Our trials never escape Him; the heavenly bandwidth is never congested.

When we die, we can expect to be greeted by the ascended Christ; He will be waiting to meet us. He arrived in heaven as our forerunner; He went ahead of us, to prepare the way.

We don't have to win on Earth in order to win in heaven; we don't have to receive glory on Earth in order to receive glory in heaven.

In this day of racial tension, we must remember that Christ has created a transnational community that will include believers of all ethnicities and races. "Worthy are you to take the scroll and to open its seals, for you were slain, and by your blood you ransomed people for God from every tribe and language and people and nation, and you have made them a kingdom and priests to our God, and they shall reign on the earth" (Revelation 5:9–10).

And there is more.

Pause and imagine this promise if you can, "The one who conquers, I will grant him to sit with me on my throne, as I also conquered and sat down with my Father on his throne." (Revelation 3:21). I don't know how big the throne of Jesus is but it's wide enough for all the saints to sit on it with Him!

Christ takes us from the mud and invites us to walk on marble; He takes us from the pit and invites us to walk in the palace. No other religion brings us so low and exalts us so high.

Girolamo Savonarola gained fame as a preacher in Florence trying to clean up the city's morals. He also predicted a flood of judgment would come upon the city if it didn't repent. He attacked the lax, corrupt citizens through fiery preaching and censorship. During the Shrove Tuesday festival in 1497, he orchestrated "a bonfire of the vanities," a ceremony where people brought their gambling artifacts, lewd books, and cosmetics to be burned.

He was excommunicated for refusing to stop preaching against the pope. He was later tried for heresy and burned. Despite the reversals he experienced, and though the truth did not triumph in his day, before his death he is to have said, "He who believes that Christ rules above, need not fear what happens below!"

C.S. Lewis was right when he said that the Christians who did the most for the present world were those who thought most of the next. "It is since Christians have largely ceased to think of the other world that they have become so ineffective in this. Aim at Heaven and you will get earth 'thrown in': aim at earth and you will get neither."[2]

Others have walked before us in the fight for truth, justice, and the proclamation of the gospel. Malcolm Muggeridge is believed to have said, "All news is old news happening to new people." There is nothing happening in the world that is news to God; it is all old news known from before the foundation of the world. Christ reigns in heaven today, fully in charge of our fallen world. And although we do not yet see all things under His feet, that day is ever closer. Those who believe that He reigns from heaven need not fear what happens on Earth.

As Americans proceed from election to election, from one political crisis to another, as we choose those whom we deem the best among imperfect political candidates, we should not lose hope. If our preferred party loses, we need to remember that we do not have to triumph in this life in order to triumph in the next. We simply need to be faithful in doing what God has asked of us. One thing that is certain is the final victory of our Leader and our God. Goodbye to the city of man; welcome to the Eternal City of God.

Take heart.

To paraphrase Peter Marshall, "it is better to fail in that which will ultimately succeed than to succeed in that which shall eventually fail." Better to fail while fighting for the

City of God, than to succeed promoting the city of man. Better to save one's soul, than to gain the whole world.

"The kingdom of the world has become the kingdom of our Lord and of his Christ, and he shall reign forever and ever" (Revelation 11:15).

Our politicians will all step aside when the King of kings comes to rule.

Footnotes

1. C.S. Lewis, *The Weight of Glory,* (New York: HarperOne, 2015), 46.
2. C.S. Lewis, "Mere Christianity," *The Complete C.S. Lewis Signature Classics* (New York: HarperOne, 2007), 112.

Made in the USA
Columbia, SC
12 February 2020

87785341R00085